THE WHITE DESERT

Noel Barber

THE WHITE DESERT

Thomas Y. Crowell Company   Established 1834   New York

We are indebted to Harcourt, Brace and Co., Inc. for their kind permission to use the extracts which appear on pages 10–11, 36, 91, and 91–92 from *Operation Deepfreeze* © 1957 by George J. Dufek.

Contents

Illustrations

THE WHITE DESERT

1. Man and Antarctica

"POLAR exploration," wrote Mr. Cherry-Garrard, "is at once the cleanest and most isolated way of having a bad time that has yet been devised."

This eminent explorer might have added with truth that it is also the most gruelling way yet devised of thoroughly enjoying oneself, and reaching the richest spiritual rewards, since it embraces not only the hazards and satisfactions of all normal exploration, but also of those two mystical challenges that have ever lured men to victory or death: the mountain, the desert.

In Antarctica the desert is white but the emotional appeal of its emptiness is as great as if it were brown, and no man who has lived from choice in its utter loneliness, flanked by its vivid mountains, can fail to enjoy it in the fullest sense of the word. Virtually unchanged since the ice age, Antarctica is the last resort of yesterday in the world of tomorrow; and because of this, it is the earth's last toehold for that restless, divided, dissatisfied, often defeated member of the human species, the practical dreamer.

There is no time or place in most of our workaday world for the dreamers of yesterday, for the Lawrences of Arabia who would not even be welcome nowadays unless they held the rank of ambassador arriving with an agreement for foreign aid. There is no room for the Byrons fighting for a good cause, lost or otherwise, for the Americans or the Russians take up the cause en masse. There are few places left to explorers that are not in part bound up with the trammels of civilization.

Alone and apart, defiant and inexorable, Antarctica beckons to the mystic. For the man who cannot dream, for the explorer with no soul, it is a white hell. But for the visionary it is a white heaven, and it is no fortuitous accident that makes the same men return time and again to its pitiless wastes, some of them to master a few of its secrets, many of them to die.

Yet no form of peaceful human endeavour demands so much of man as life in Antarctica. The jungle paths of Africa, the mountain passes of China all have their perils, but man always knows that somewhere around him is life, even if hostile. A dusty shrub, the cry of an animal, a sudden splash of green grass can lend delight to men who do not even know if they will ever reach journey's end. Antarctica has none of these. It is lonely, dead, cruel, inhospitable, and irresistible. No breath of life clouds it. It has no animal to befriend one, no reptile to frighten, no insect to annoy; not even a spider to lend courage and set example.

It has nothing of life, but it is clean, and perhaps because of this it is the last corner of our world where all adventure is clothed in the magic of the spirit. Because it is lifeless it is still of the ice age, so that man who travels to the bottom of the world is also travelling back in time. It is this, this extra dimension, that has made men like Scott and Shackleton, Byrd and Dufek, lose their hearts and their souls to Antarctica, so that always they await only the opportunity of returning to its savage isolation and deem themselves lucky to be afforded the honor. To these names now must be added a new one: Vivian Fuchs, endowed with all the special qualities which Antarctica demands, but which are required all too infrequently in ordinary life. Courage, patience, endurance, yes; but there are many who have these in sufficient quantity to match their wits against Antarctica's unyielding ferocity. More is required; a spiritual quality, a quality of mysticism. A man does not say, even to himself, "I will go and explore Antarctica because it seems like a good idea." Nor does the man crossed in love decide to forget all in an attempt to reach the South Pole.

The man who goes to Antarctica goes because he cannot help it, because the forces that drag him away from hearth and home, into squalor and cold, are too strong for him to deny. This is a call, a desire of the spirit which has nothing vulgar about it but which is, in fact, so strong that men will forsake all—wives, children, homes, friends—to fulfil it. No mistress was ever so demanding as the seventh continent.

It is as well that these values be stated at the outset, for they may help to underline the qualities of the two chief characters in this volume, Sir Vivian Fuchs and Sir Edmund Hillary; not only their qualities, but their defects. Not only the similarities in their attitude towards Polar exploration, but the differences which caused so much controversy midway through the expedition, and upon which I shall have much to say later in this volume.

The cynic may well say that though the spiritual lure of Antarctica could apply to men like Scott and Fuchs, it has nothing to do with the hundreds of American sailors who now live in Antarctica, and this is in some degree true, but do not forget that the American sailors in Antarctica are members of the armed forces who are, in the words of Admiral Dufek, their leader, waging "the toughest operation I've ever seen, in war or peace." To many of them, duty in Antarctica may have been a depressing military chore, the soonest finished the better, but not to all; and certainly not to their leaders whose task was the unenviable one of supporting scientists, all volunteers, who had willingly chosen to live in such hostile surroundings to probe its secrets; the same reason, of course, which prompted the great journey of Dr. Fuchs.

The cynic may also say that I too did not venture into Antarctica because of an overwhelming spiritual emotion. But I am not the maker of history, I am its eyewitness. Not for me the laurels that await the conquering hero; for me there is the more mundane task of accompanying tomorrow's hero through his trials and tribulations. I go to war more often than the average man, but though I see shots fired in anger, I never fire one. Yet in my three months in Antarctica, during which time I was in such close contact with both Hillary and Fuchs, I did find, without any question whatsoever, a spiritual force denied to me in other corners of the world. I went there, to record the adventures of two great men, with no knowledge of what lay in store for me; I left almost three months later with an indefinable feeling of excitement, to which is added a secret hope that I hardly dare to admit, even to myself, that one day I may be able to return.

As Fuchs started to make his final preparations for the trek that would make world history, the last great assault on Antarctica started. The vast, trackless wastes remained as in the days of Scott and Shackleton, but dotted here and there were encampments of men who somehow managed to survive in the white desert. The fearful terrain and the terrible conditions were just the same as when Scott and Shackleton had blazed their trails. But at each lonely spot where men had chosen to live, comforts unknown to the early explorers began to appear. There was a reason for this, and this too must be clearly stated at the outset so that the scene is properly set for the great adventure that is to follow.

A long time had passed since Roald Amundsen discovered the South Pole in December 1911, and Captain Scott reached it only a month later and died on the return trip. Since then no man had reached the elusive Pole on foot, and no Englishman had been there—until with the convenience of modern aircraft, I flew there to await its two conquerors. Time and again men had tried to pierce the white shroud. Time and again they had been driven back. And long before Fuchs first dreamed of crossing the continent, another man, perhaps the greatest explorer of all, had the same dream. This was Ernest Shackleton who, in 1913, launched his audacious plan for "the last great Polar journey that can be made" in which he hoped to cross the Antarctic and "solve the complete nature of the continent." He never succeeded.

As time passed, explorers of the new age took his place, predominant among them Admiral Byrd. And to Byrd, as with Scott, Shackleton, and Fuchs, all exploration was a means to a scientific end. Unlike Hillary, with his restless soul, Byrd might have said as Fuchs said to me, "There is no point in going from A to B just for the sake of doing so." Byrd was the great explorer of the air age, and as the president of the National Geographic Society said after his death in 1957, "No man in history contributed more to the knowledge of the Arctic and Antarctic than Byrd. This year's great scientific assault on Antarctica represents the culmination of his lifetime of work and leadership."

Byrd was never to reach the South Pole either. But he did fly over it, the first man to do so, and when the Pole Station was established shortly before his death, the Admiral who could not be present asked that the station should be named the Amundsen-Scott South Pole Station, for "it is fitting that we should honor the memories of those two great and gallant men who first reached the South Pole . . . Scott lies gently shrouded in the snows he loved and so often traversed. Amundsen lies at the other end of the earth, beneath the waters of the Arctic."

Byrd made his last visit to Antarctica in 1956, and by then a new character had stepped on the scene, the first man to land by aircraft at the South Pole, Rear-Admiral George Dufek of the United States Navy, Byrd's "number two," then his successor, and another man whom the Antarctic had drawn into her spell.

Yet neither of these men, nor Fuchs either, could have undertaken their missions in Antarctica without a reason sufficiently important to warrant the great expense involved; and this reason was science.

Twice before in history scientists made a concerted effort irrespective of national bitternesses and rivalries, to collaborate in an examination of the earth's physical environment. In 1882, the First International Polar Year studied geophysical aspects of the Polar regions, and fifty years later, in 1932–33, thirty-four countries cooperated in the Second International Polar Year. Now a third international year was being prepared, the International Geophysical Year of 1957–58, by far the largest joint enterprise ever undertaken in the name of science, and actually stretching over eighteen months. The program was vast, but much of it was centered on the Polar region, where nature herself had a titanic physical, chemical, and biological laboratory unequalled in the rest of the world.

Since Fuchs made his trans-Antarctic crossing primarily in the name of science, the scientific background to his expedition and the immense efforts made by other nations are important. It was the backdrop to his trek, the scene in which he acted out his part, a drama of hundreds of characters, working as assiduously as he did, taking the same grave risks, to explore as never before the forces of our earth.

To the explorers whose only goal was Antarctica—to men like Fuchs who had dreamed of this journey for more than 20 years—science offered the perfect opportunity for a speedy marriage with exploration, for the scientific studies could never have been carried out without men to build bases in the midst of this icy wilderness. Much had to be done. Bases had to be established, supplies flown in to Antarctica. For the most part men would fly from point to point, but in this flying age, Dr. Fuchs had at last his great chance to study science in the grand manner of yesterday, on foot, alone, taking years to bring to a successful climax the most arduous journey the world has ever known.

While Fuchs was trying to raise funds, and later planning the expedition, the IGY started to take preliminary shape. It had always been the great brainchild of Byrd, but now Byrd was too old to take part except from afar, and so Dufek stepped in, the man of action, who deserves the greatest possible credit for the real opening up of Antarctica. Only two countries—the United States and Soviet Russia—had sufficient money to build, equip, and even more maintain a large number of bases—the only two countries, incidentally, which do not recognise the territorial claims to Antarctica made by other nations.

Many of the suggested sites presented only problems of logistics and finance, but there was one that had an extra problem attached to it: the South Pole. No man had reached the Pole by land or air since Scott, but one day surely it would be "inhabited." The United States decided it would be more politic for their country to set up a station there—an IGY station in the first instance—than the Russians. To have had the Russians sitting at the South Pole would have been a bitter blow to Western pride.

But could a plane land there? It could. At 8:34 P.M. on October 31, 1956, Admiral Dufek landed at the South Pole in a twin-engined DC3 piloted by Commander Gus Shinn, and planted the Stars and Stripes at the bottom of the world. From that moment America knew it was only a question of time to fly in ten, twenty, or a hundred planes, tons of material, and equip and maintain a scientific base there. The trip would always be hazardous and difficult, but it could be done, and done again.

The Americans never waste time, and only three weeks later construction of the South Pole base started, when U.S. Navy planes put down an advance party of eight men on the plateau and Globemasters started parachuting building materials and supplies.

Everything was to be supplied by air; because of the erratic landing conditions, most of it would be parachuted down. To support the Pole, and other scientific stations, a base had to be built at McMurdo Sound, the front door to Antarctica. Even this presented tremendous difficulties. From Christchurch in New Zealand to McMurdo Sound was 2,230 miles, with no alternative landing grounds over Antarctic water where no man can live for more than eight minutes. No wonder the project was called "Operation Deepfreeze."

When the Navy started planning the Pole Station in 1955–56 Dufek had to work out the cost and he asked for 58 million dollars.

President Eisenhower cut it to 22 million dollars and told Dufek
to do the best he could. Today the Pole Station with its comple-
ment of eighteen men costs about 1 million dollars per man per
year according to Paul Siple, first scientific leader to spend a winter
there.

With astonishing speed, three thousand Americans descended
on the Antarctic continent and started to prepare the way for the
IGY year soon to begin. By the time Fuchs was prepared to start,
Antarctica was more than ready for the scientists so eager to discover its secrets.

Ten nations settled down in the Antarctic stations to work
there until the IGY should end on December 31, 1958. Their
main studies centered around terrestrial magnetism, the ionosphere, polar radiation, cosmic rays, and the influence of Antarctic
weather on the rest of the world's weather. With this, scientists
were studying in great detail and for the first time the effects of
cold weather living on human beings and on the metals of their
machines.

Britain had two major contributions, the most important being the Royal Society's Halley Bay Base, with the Trans-Antarctic
Expedition running it a close second in scientific importance.
America had seven bases, with McMurdo as its main logistics base
where stores were to be landed before being flown to other bases.
The station known as Little America, on the Ross Ice Shelf, was
the most important scientifically, with the Pole second in scientific
importance and first in political significance. Among the other
bases which I was to visit there was even a petrol filling station
manned by three men at the foot of the Beardmore Glacier, 400
miles from the nearest man.

Russia had five bases, with Mirny the most important. It was
one of the biggest bases in the Antarctic continent. With Mirny
as their base, the Russians had sent off a tractor train of 10 tractors, 20 sledges and 30 men to try and set up a base at the "Pole
of Inaccessibility," the point in Antarctica furthest removed from

the coast, while a Soviet air party formed a base named Vostok near the magnetic pole.

The other nations taking part were New Zealand, Belgium, Australia, Argentina, Chile, France, Japan, and Norway. New Zealand had an expedition quite separate from the small force under Sir Edmund Hillary whose task was to lend support to Dr. Fuchs. The main scientific party of New Zealanders was among other things exploring the Ross Sea Dependency for minerals, while another team was searching for a strange Antarctic area where the glaciers had retreated leaving valleys with that unusual phenomenon, no ice and snow. Australia maintained three bases, Argentina four, France two.

The greatest work of all in this year of Antarctica fell to the Americans; the greatest adventure to the British. But above all, the IGY was a great international team effort in which every man played a part, and into that year, Dr. Siple said, were being telescoped decades of normal research, with findings that would affect the lives of people all over the world.

The cost to the Americans was great. One icebreaker lost a propellor, another its propellor shaft. I saw a third stuck in the ice with its bows ripped open and frantic men, working at thirty below, welding steel plates to the buckled sheets of metal. An oil tanker was crushed between two ice floes and as her seams opened she spilled nearly 150,000 gallons of aviation fuel. Damage to ships in the vital four months of preparation cost $300,000. The flying hazards were even worse, for the flight to establish the Pole station was never routine and still is not. Six aircraft were taken from the active Polar list, including damage to three giant Globemasters costing a million pounds each; one of the carcasses in the snow was my only view for weeks without end at McMurdo. The logistical difficulties were fantastic, and quite apart from food and equipment, 42 per cent of all the space in cargo ships going to Antarctica was being used for fuel while the bases were being established. Now that they are established, and the operation is one of resupply, the cargo space required for fuel has risen to 70 per cent.

The IGY was not confined to the Polar regions, and, in all, 64 nations planned to spend about $420 million for research during the 18 months of the "year" that started at midnight on June 30, 1957. A large proportion of the effort and money was being spent on the Polar regions, not only to make up for any lack of knowledge of the least explored part of the earth, but because of their special positions. Not only is Antarctica the ice reserve of the world (and therefore in a sense the water reserve) but also the center of several phenomena that affect even now our daily lives. In the sphere of physical science much is hard to understand, but in nonscientific language, the scientific work of the IGY in Antarctica was best summed up in Admiral Dufek's book *Operation Deepfreeze*:

"The answers to many questions will be sought. Is there a relationship between sunspots and solar flares and long-range radio transmission? What causes the aurora? What is the nature of cosmic rays and where do they come from? Are we in a changing cycle of weather? Is the earth warming or cooling? Are glaciers receding?

"Several studies will undoubtedly influence our rocket program: meteorology—a knowledge of the wind system (velocity and direction) above the stratosphere is necessary for navigation of missiles, and of the density of the atmosphere because it will determine the type of metal casing for the rocket. Magnetism . . . is important to guidance systems which may be affected by the distribution of the earth's magnetic forces; ionosphere—information is needed to determine day-to-day fluctuations of its layers because they influence radio waves, and with a guidance system using radio waves, this would be extremely important; cosmic rays —a study of these rays influenced by solar activity . . . will serve as the basis for all operational procedures in guided missiles, etc.

"The weather has always played an important part in the life of man throughout the advance of civilization. It influences his manner of living, the construction of his shelter, his production and commerce, and the food he eats. Early and reliable reporting of weather, and if possible its control, has been the objective of meteorologists throughout the years. Weather is a global entity. To understand the whole it is necessary to have knowledge of each part. The part that has been missing in the past has been knowledge of the remote regions of the southern hemisphere, especially Antarctica.

"During the IGY, nearly 65 stations will be established in the Antarctic and the surrounding areas. For the first time in the history of man scientists will attempt to construct daily weather maps of this huge continent and surrounding oceans. Thus the missing link in a world weather map will be fitted into the pattern. It will probably be possible to predict the weather all over the world more accurately and further in advance. A few dreamers even look forward to the day when it may be possible to control the weather. Such men foresee fresh water that falls on the oceans —three-fifths of the earth's surface—may be diverted to the Sahara desert, the dust bowls of the United States and other arid land. Agriculture would flourish in now barren lands. Food could be plentiful for all.

"Here in the Antarctic we have the opportunity to help remove the causes that breed wars. We can use the tools developed to prosecute wars to build bases and support the scientists in order that they may unlock the secrets of our universe."

To find these answers, all kinds of strange scientific instruments were taken to Antarctica, ranging from ingenious cameras (called the Gartlein All-Sky Camera) which took pictures of the entire sky every five minutes to provide a continuous record, to pink dye which was injected into penguin eggs so that, when hatched, the colored down of the birds would make it easier to track them and study their behavior.

Seismology, in which the Fuchs expedition was to concentrate, would give the world the first accurate picture of the contours of the Antarctic continent. This work alone was of major help to the

Americans who were trying to map Antarctica by aerial photography. Fuchs, and Fuchs alone, was to give the Americans enough information to turn their flat aerial photographs into photographs in depth.

To correlate this scientific knowledge, without which it would have been valueless, the IGY conceived the "IGY Calendar" which named three days in each month as "World Days." On these days, complicated observations were made all over the world, synchronised to the exact second to give scientists a complete world picture of physical forces affecting the earth at the same time.

Was it all worth it? There are two answers, both of which come from the voices of other men. I sat drinking whisky at the Pole one night with George Dufek, a strange blend of the practical and the idealist, a man of great personal courage and integrity, and when I asked him that question, as we awaited the arrival of Fuchs from South Ice, he said to me, "If the IGY finds the answers to its questions, it will affect almost every field of human activity—shipping, construction, air travel, agriculture, radio communications, navigation. You know, scientists will never admit how much their findings are worth, but one eminent scientist told me that the work in the Antarctic these 18 months will be worth a billion dollars to the free world's rocket programme. Rocket powered commercial space ships will be able to fly round the world in three hours. All of us here—you and I, Noel, and Bunny Fuchs on the trail—are in at the turning point of space knowledge."

And there was another, even more fundamental reason which the Polar explorer Fridtjof Nansen gave for man's restless quest after knowledge. It is of no purpose, he believed, to discuss the use of knowledge. Man wants to know and when he ceases to be curious, he will no longer be man.

Into this great field of adventure, there slowly moved the puny, magnificent, impertinent effort of Vivian Fuchs, determined to cross the world's last frontier for the first time in history.

This volume, with its background of scientific work of a dozen or more nations, is about that last great journey and the indomitable man who made it. It is a tale of a conquest, of lonely men struggling from opposite ends of the continent in fulfilment of one man's dream; an adventure so out of tune with the age of the airplane that many people must have asked "Why on earth go on foot when you can fly? What's the point of it?" Yet it was to prove a journey of infinite value not only to science but to the spirit of adventure which is what makes man man.

But this tale is more than that, for it is also the story of two strange and restless men, Fuchs and Hillary, so similar in courage, so different in character; differences that caused bitter feeling between the two explorers that no platitudinous phrases can cover up. In the following pages, the characters of these two men will reveal themselves, as they were revealed to me from my curious vantage point between the two of them; and in these pages will be answered too, I hope, some of the questions which Dr. Fuchs has refrained from dwelling upon in his own account of the journey.

Was Hillary right to go to the Pole? Had he planned it before in secret or was it an unpremeditated dash? And once Hillary had reached the Pole, did Fuchs really ask him to stay, wait for him then guide him back across the plateau? If so, why did Hillary refuse? Had Fuchs and Hillary quarrelled before?

Inevitably with two such contrasting characters, all these questions arise and there are answers to each of them. Yet the personal differences in no way detract from the magnificence of the achievement, for this was no film with carefully delineated characters, this was a chunk of life in the raw lived by men with normal defects as well as bravery.

In a very small way, my own part is portrayed in this volume too. It was not heroic, but since both of these great explorers reached the South Pole, I think it is proper that, with my greater length of time there, I should give my personal impressions of what this strange little white oasis was like, how it was maintained, and what Fuchs and Hillary found on their arrivals there. I had too, as part of the general picture of Antarctica, considerable experience of flying, which though far less arduous than the work of Fuchs and Hillary, may still have given me impressions which complete the picture.

But the book in truth is the story of the Expedition, of the great dangers that beset it, of the drama in human relationships and, above all, the story of Bunny Fuchs.

His road was a lonely one, the kind of road that thwarted Shackleton's great ambition, that cost Scott his death a few miles only from safety. As I followed the bitter adventures of Fuchs, I thought often of Scott, after he had conquered the Beardmore, moving across the gently rising plateau to the Pole, and in his tent one night entering into his diary these words:

"We see only a few miles of ruffled snow, bounded by a vague wavy horizon, but we know that beyond that horizon are hundreds and even thousands of miles which can offer no change to the weary eye . . . One knows there is neither tree, nor shrub, nor any living thing, nor even inanimate rock—nothing but this terrible limitless expanse of snow. It has been so for countless years, and it will be so for countless more. And we, little human insects, have started to crawl over this awful desert . . . Could anything be more terrible than this silent, wind-swept immensity?"

Scott was to die. But Fuchs was to live with the glory and to add his share to human knowledge. It was my privilege to see this being done, and to watch the adventure unfold, perhaps more than any other man, for I saw it from both sides—as one trail of "little human insects" crawled from the Weddell Sea and another from the Ross Sea. And I saw too the characters of the men in this splendid love affair between adventure and science, and the courage of one who was determined to carry on to the end—Fuchs, long under the spell of Antarctica's mystic attraction which, as Byrd wrote ten years previously, "sirenlike challenges the restless, adventure-hungry postwar world."

2. The Birth of the Trans-Antarctic Expedition

THE time was 1948, the place Graham Land, Antarctica. Here, when Fuchs was leader of the Falkland Islands Dependencies Survey, a violent blizzard sprung up with all the sudden ferocity that makes Antarctica's weather the most savage in the world. It was impossible for men, the only living creatures for thousands of miles around, to move, and for three days Fuchs was trapped in his tent, the only blob of color in the swirling white storm. Three days is a long time to be cooped up, huddled in a sleeping bag for warmth, cooking alone, digging snow under the tent walls to heat and melt for drinking water, with the flaps of the tent fastened tightly, cutting one off from the world outside, however hostile; a time for boredom, a time for depression; or a time for making dreams come true.

This was the moment in the life of Fuchs when the hopes he had nursed for so long moved, in his mind, from the shadow world of an impossible dream to the arena of practical possibility; the moment when he knew he could do it, the moment when he knew he would do it. The dream of crossing Antarctica had been conceived many years previously, but this was the moment when it was really born.

For over twenty years Fuchs had dreamed of making the trans-Antarctic trip where Shackleton had failed. His wife has told how he even took maps and books about the South Pole on their honeymoon twenty-three years ago and how, even then, he mapped out the very same route he was eventually to follow. But during those three lonely days in his sleeping bag, he first visualised the trek and the way it could be brought about. It would need a great deal of money, powerful backing, and much time, too. And time meant patience. Fuchs himself knew that he was equipped for the task, but that would not be enough, for explorers and scientists are not immune from human jealousies and rivalries that affect less noble callings. Fuchs was going to find it almost as hard to start the expedition as to end it. But in fact, both the start in 1948, and the end ten years later, demanded of Fuchs the same qualities—philosophy in the face of setbacks, a determination not to surrender, and incalculable patience.

Vivian Ernest Fuchs was born on February 11, 1908, the son of a German who emigrated to England at the age of seven and became a prosperous farmer. The son was educated at Brighton College and St. John's College, Cambridge, a choice which had much to do with Fuchs' passion for exploring, for there in 1929, he went on his first expedition with Sir James Wordie, then a tutor of St. John's, to Greenland.

Throughout the years, Fuchs and Wordie used to talk about the dream of a trans-Antarctic crossing, and finally it was Wordie, the father of British exploration, who lent the powerful support necessary to start Fuchs off. Sir James, now Master of St. John's, had been chief scientist with Shackleton's expedition; he has a glacier named after him in Greenland, and as one friend put it, "At Cambridge, Fuchs used to spend all his spare time planning the expedition with Wordie."

Fuchs went abroad. He made one trip exploring Africa. He spent three years at a stretch in Antarctica—one year more than planned when the relief ship *John Briscoe* which was to bring him and his party back to England could not force a passage through the pack ice. Fuchs had to stay another winter before being relieved—and calmly settled down to more scientific work.

But all the time he and Wordie kept in touch, when they could. And as soon as Fuchs returned from Antarctica he made posthaste to see his old tutor and friend at Cambridge and told him the time was ripe to go ahead. Wordie promised to do everything he could to help. Before long Fuchs was made director of the Falkland Island Dependencies Scientific Bureau, a post which finally showed the measure of his skills both as an "old Antarctic hand" and as a scientist.

Fuchs and Wordie went into action—and came up against immediate and bitter opposition to his plans. The Scott Polar Research Institute treated the proposed expedition as a joke. There were many who thought it impossible to set up a base on the Weddell Sea coast where Shackleton's ship, the *Endurance*, had been crushed in the ice (and where Fuchs almost met disaster before the crossing proper started). But Sir James Wordie wielded great power behind the scenes—the more so because he believed passionately that where Shackleton had failed in crossing Antarctica, another man could succeed given courage, modern machines, air support—and money.

In the end it was the greatest living Englishman who gave Bunny Fuchs his chance. In 1954, four years after returning from Antarctica, Fuchs met Churchill. He told him the whole story, of the opposition, of the possibilities, both of failure and success—in the shy, diffident manner which belies so much of Fuchs' determination. Churchill was so impressed he arranged for Fuchs to tell his story again to the Conference of Commonwealth Prime Ministers. At that historic meeting, Fuchs literally sold the idea to the world; for he came away with pledged financial support. Sir Winston promised him £100,000 from the British Government. New Zealand offered £50,000, South Africa £18,000. Shortly afterwards, *The Times* and the BBC offered substantial sums for the journalistic and broadcasting rights, and public subscriptions were started to bring the figure up to the half million mark.

It was very little by modern counting methods, but it was just enough to see him through with 16 men, ten tracked vehicles, two dog teams, two single-engined aircraft and Hillary's support party, which planned to go out from the other side of Antarctica and prove the last 700 miles of the 2,000 mile route. Fuchs set about choosing a team of volunteers, to whom he offered flat salaries of £10 each a week. Many had to relinquish well-paid jobs for the journey, yet Fuchs insisted that they sign away all their book, newspaper and lecture rights for two years after their return. He had no shortage of men aching to go with him.

Early in 1955, a London committee was formed under the chairmanship of Sir John Slessor, and a scientific subcommittee made the first approach to the RAF for the air support so necessary to the expedition.

A year of intensive work lay ahead of Fuchs, for until now, he was almost on his own. He knew exactly the route he planned to take, he knew exactly how he wanted the expedition to be undertaken, he knew what kind of men he wanted; but finding the men, organising the complex facets of such a large-scale expedition took nearly twelve months.

Once again, though, time did not matter. The expedition was guaranteed, and Fuchs knew he was going to attempt the historic crossing. He had waited years before gaining the necessary support. Another year or two of waiting were quite unimportant, particularly if that time could be profitably employed in planning the trek down to the last detail, and in rugged training of the men when selected.

Mrs. Fuchs (a remarkable woman in her own right who had made a journey alone round the world before her marriage in 1943) summed up Fuchs' contempt for time by saying, "This wasn't a quick boyish adventure. My husband has carried this idea through his life. . . ."

But there was much work to be done before this.

By early 1955, with the hope that the advance party could sail for the Weddell Sea later in the year, Fuchs had chosen his first four men. David Stratton was appointed deputy leader and in charge of stores, and to him fell the gigantic task of writing to all the firms who would supply material for the expedition; for though large sums had been promised, Fuchs had, as *The Observer* pointed out, "to plan his expedition in a typically British way" with contributions from manufacturers and suppliers as well as cash grants.

Stratton was to prove a great strength to Fuchs right from the start of the planning. At the same time David Pratt was chosen for the engineering side, while George Lowe, Hillary's friend from Everest and the only New Zealander up to that time, handled publicity and public appeals for funds. From the RAF came Squadron Leader John Lewis, one of the force's greatest Antarctic pilots, whose courage is only matched by his experience. Lewis was to make an historic flight from South Ice to Scott Base in a single-engined aircraft. The fact that he made it wearing a top hat only added to the luster. Fuchs let Lewis choose his men for the air support party, and as Fuchs became more and more snowed under with the paper work of the expedition, Lewis flew to Canada to order the aircraft.

By mid-1955, the planning was well under way, and by then Hillary had agreed to lead the New Zealand support party.

No two men could be more different from each other. Hillary was 6 feet 4 inches, tall and rangy, a rough diamond with a rough diamond's attitude to life, ready when annoyed to express himself extremely forcibly. Fuchs was stocky, deceptively shy in manner, quiet, polished, almost suave. Later, after the Pole dash, Hillary, increasingly anxious about spending the winter in Antarctica, was never afraid to make criticisms of the way Fuchs was behind schedule; but though Fuchs may have been bitterly upset at the publicity given to their differences, I never heard him criticise Hillary in the slightest.

The differences in character were even more profound. Antarctica demands, above all else from a man, the quality of patience. Fuchs had it to an astonishing degree. Hillary didn't. Douglas Liversidge, the author, who was in the vessel *John Briscoe* which rescued Fuchs after he had been cut off for a year in Antarctica in 1948, said that when his vessel arrived, "none of the men showed any depression, yet here is Hillary after a few months in Antarctica complaining about the monotony." Mr. Liversidge thought, as many Antarctic experts did, that "it would have been a better choice to have somebody with great Antarctic experience to lead the supporting party instead of Hillary, men who are attuned to loneliness and wouldn't have become bored like Hillary."

This fundamental difference in character was inevitable since one man was a scientist and the other an explorer. While to Fuchs, brought up under the wing of Sir James Wordie, science was a major reason for the expedition, Hillary was basically un-interested in science. He regarded Fuchs' interminable seismic soundings as one more way of slowing up the adventure, and was not afraid to say so. I am quite certain also (as this book will show) that while Fuchs had never thought of the South Pole as anything more than a point to be reached on the way across Antarctica, Hillary, from the moment he agreed to work with Fuchs, hoped secretly that he might reach the Pole. Instinctively he knew the great *réclame* such a dash would make, a dash which fitted in perfectly with the restless energy of a man who regarded every obstacle with personal hostility, and as a challenge to be overcome at the first opportunity before moving on to the next one.

Both had points in common—resolution, great courage, amazing powers of endurance; but there the similarities end. Perhaps Fuchs chose Hillary because he knew that, above all, Hillary was a very brave man with the strength of an ox; and also he was a New Zealander, and it was a happy thought that the leader of the support party should come from the country that did so much, and gave so much, towards the success of the enterprise.

By November 1955, plans had sufficiently progressed for an advance party led by Fuchs to leave for Antarctica, where eight men would spend the winter completing a base to be known as Shackleton, while Fuchs would return to London. Fuchs chartered an ice ship called the *Theron*, 829 tons, for the journey to the Weddell Sea, at a cost of £275 a day. She was a fine little vessel, as she needed to be for the Weddell Sea, built in Glasgow especially for work in the ice pack, and had been operating as a sealer in the Canadian Arctic. The *Theron* planned to stop at Montevideo to pick up Hillary and Squadron Leader John Claydon of the New Zealand RAF, who would be in charge of air operations from the New Zealand Scott Base when it was established later on McMurdo Sound. Fuchs thought it a good idea that they should have some Antarctic training on the Weddell Sea coast as well.

The eight men chosen to spend the first winter establishing the Shackleton base were the four men originally chosen by Fuchs, plus the second batch of four he had picked: Ken Blaiklock, a surveyor and dog handler, who would be in charge of the winter party, Hannes La Grange, meteorologist from South Africa, Taffy Williams of the RAF, in charge of radio, and Ralph Lenton, who would be in charge of base construction, but also qualified in radio.

Even this preliminary task—to be undertaken long before the crossing proper—was a formidable one, for the Weddell Sea had the most treacherous ice pack of all Antarctica.

It was here in 1915 that Shackleton's *Endurance* was crushed by the ice. Shackleton and his men drifted for nearly fifteen months in the ice pack, moving almost 1,500 miles until finally they took to small boats and reached Elephant Island in the South Shetlands. From there, in one of Antarctica's most dramatic voyages, Shackleton sailed another 800 miles for help in a 22-foot whaleboat, reaching South Georgia Island and bringing back rescuers for the men he had left behind.

This was the scene that awaited Fuchs when he set off for the

Weddell Sea, and the little *Theron* sailed down the Thames with an incredible variety of stores, ranging from crackers for the midwinter "Christmas Day"—Midsummer's Day in Britain—to the first of the three ton Sno-Cats that would finally cross the continent. The vessel also carried two light aircraft, two Weasels, and twenty-four huskies.

Fuchs knew the Weddell Sea and all the dangers that awaited him there, but he hoped that with the help of John Lewis flying a light aircraft, it would be possible to search out routes ahead in the ice pack. But it was touch and go. Lewis was able on occasion to give the *Theron* a sure route, but the ice shifted so rapidly and built up so quickly that the tiny ship was delayed time after time. This delay very nearly cost the expedition disaster when it had hardly started, for it delayed the arrival of the *Theron* at the Weddell Sea coast by nearly three weeks—a critical three weeks during the comparatively short Antarctic summer.

When the *Theron* finally reached the ice cliffs that mark the edge of the continent, they had other problems to face. In some parts the cliffs were 100 feet high, in others only 15 feet. Lewis was entrusted with the task of finding the most favourable spot at which to land the stores; and, as Fuchs said, "We are prepared to get our equipment ashore anywhere on cliffs up to a height of 30 feet."

The *Theron* carried a supply of telegraph poles so that, if necessary, Fuchs could make a bridge that would slope from the deck of the *Theron* to the cliff tops and be strong enough for the Sno-Cat to trundle across; this they arranged to do on a stretch of the solid ice-coast picked out from the ice cliffs of the Weddell Sea that were often floating on top of the sea and frequently split away.

The advance party landed safely in the Antarctic high summer, and pitched their tents. All set to work to start building the base as quickly as possible.

Then disastrous weather really struck the tiny camp, with such ferocity that almost all the stores remaining had to be landed from the *Theron* in less than a week, while the party watched the ice literally closing in on them and threatening to crush their ship as it had crushed the *Endurance* forty years before. This was a disaster that had to be beaten.

Already, the *Theron* had been trapped in the ice pack for three weeks while the armchair critics in London who had opposed Fuchs did not disguise their delight that the Weddell Sea, which had beaten Shackleton, had also—so they thought—beaten Fuchs. Now it looked as though she would be trapped for the winter, and at £275 a day that could have meant the end financially of the Trans-Antarctic Expedition. Fuchs himself told of its most hazardous moments. "Our plan was to stay as long as we dared, to advance the construction of a hut for the eight men in the wintering party," he said, "but luck was against us. On February 10 a 60-knot blizzard struck. It was pretty awful. Visibility was down to a matter of feet. The wind began blowing water in over the ice. Our stores were flooded and some of the boxes began floating away. We had to wade knee deep to rescue them. As quickly as possible we began trying to get them to higher ground. We had to put up posts every 50 feet to guide us."

Fuchs had planned to build Shackleton base at a point 120 feet above sea level, Vahsel Bay, on ice 1,000 feet thick, and so bad was the blizzard that, according to Fuchs, "The party up at the base side knew nothing of our difficulties. Then the wind began to pull at the *Theron* and the stern cables holding her to the ice broke. The ship disappeared from view. We carried on rescuing stores and half an hour later the *Theron* loomed up. I ordered everybody on board. The ship laid off for twenty-four hours and then came back and we started work again."

The decision to leave came soon afterwards. Ken Blaiklock was flying in one of the expedition aircraft that had been safely unloaded when he saw vast floes of ice coming in and free water beginning to freeze. "We didn't dare to stay any longer," said Fuchs. "When this particular condition comes about, even an icebreaker cannot get through. I gave orders to pull out as soon as the last few bits of stores had been unloaded. I apologized to Blaiklock for having to leave him and his boys with so much work to do. We had hoped to have the living-hut partially completed."

But nothing was completed. The expedition was having its first lesson (as though Fuchs needed it) in the contrariness of the Antarctic weather, the force that rules every life. Firstly the pack had delayed the *Theron* so that she was three weeks later than expected in arriving. Then Fuchs had hoped to stay in Antarctica until around the end of March—yet the ice was so dangerous he had to pull out in mid-February.

The eight men were left behind—with virtually nothing started and with the prospect of winter ahead. But the weather had not finished with them yet and what had happened was nothing to what was to follow.

When Fuchs sailed away—and what a moment that must have been for the eight men against the ice!—they set about building a temporary shelter by reassembling the crate of a Sno-Cat as their "living room" while using four double-skinned tents for sleeping, two to a tent. Once the Sno-Cat room was up, the party started to erect the wall sections of their main hut. Then another blizzard struck this featureless extremity of the Weddell Sea ice shelf. The main hut—or what was built of it—vanished overnight under drifts of snow twenty feet deep. The Sno-Cat hut miraculously withstood the tempest, but then, as the men came out of their tents to see what they could save from the ruins, the sea ice broke up, and in one despairing moment the eight men saw almost all their stores carried away to sea. All their coal, almost all their paraffin for heating, two huts, a tractor—all vanished to sea. The eight men with winter already upon them were left with food, four tents, and the crate—twenty feet by eight feet and seven feet high.

There was nothing that anybody could do for them, no hope of reaching them until the following November. The walls and the ceiling of the crate were covered with frost, the ventilators were blocked, and sometimes the air inside was so heavy with carbon dioxide that the men could not even light matches. They suffered from violent headaches and vomiting. The thermometer went down to minus 64 degrees, and the wind up to 75 knots. Blaiklock estimated that the eight men shovelled more than 120 tons of snow by hand out of the one building they were able slowly to erect in these primitive conditions.

Meanwhile, the *Theron* had returned to London. Hillary flew home to select his party and start training in the New Zealand Alps. Fuchs went ahead with the last details before leaving again for Shackleton, where he too would spend a winter of training before actually starting the adventure at the beginning of the Antarctic summer late in 1957.

In mid-November 1956, Fuchs sailed from London for the Weddell Sea in a Danish ice ship, the *Magga Dan*. A month later Hillary set off from New Zealand in a wooden vessel called the *Endeavour*, but which was in fact the good old *John Briscoe*, which had rescued Fuchs after his three years in Antarctica and, on being acquired for the expedition, had been renamed.

Fuchs had now completed his party, with Jon Stephenson, of Australia, as a geologist; Geoffrey Pratt (no relation of David), seismologist; Hal Lister, glaciologist; and Allan Rogers, medical officer.

Both vessels arrived in Antarctica about the same time. On both sides of the white desert, the men were ready for action. But it was to be nearly a year before the trek really started.

The New Zealanders established Scott Base and started proving the route across the Ross Ice Shelf towards the Skelton Glacier. Scott Base, only two miles from the American base of McMurdo, on Ross Island, became a cozy, warm, and hospitable home from home. It even had a post office of its own with its postmaster. (When I asked whether I could send a private telegram to my wife from Scott Base, one expedition member said "Sure—ask the postmaster. He'll fix it for you." Then he bowed to the postmaster. It was Hillary, legally invested with this title by the New Zealand authorities.) All members of the New Zealand team wintered over at Scott Base.

At Shackleton, Fuchs faced one big problem. All his knowledge, backed now by aerial reconnaissance, suggested that by far the
most difficult portion of his trip would be the initial run from Shackleton to South Ice (originally called Depot 300), a point 270 miles
from Shackleton on the route to the South Pole. In February Fuchs
flew over the terrain to select the best route to South Ice, where he
proposed to establish an advance depot with fuel for John Lewis,
so that he could fly directly from South Ice to Scott when eventually
Fuchs had passed this point on his trek proper.

A hut was established at South Ice, and it was decided to leave
three men there to occupy it for the Antarctic winter. Here again
near-disaster almost overtook the expedition before it had really
started. Two of the men wintering at South Ice, Blaiklock and
Stephenson, were lost for twelve days in a blizzard while doing scientific work in temperatures down to minus 52 degrees, near South
Ice. For eleven days the weather was so bad that no flying was possible, but on the twelfth Fuchs flew out in a high wind with Lewis
and, ten miles from South Ice, in a sudden miraculous break in the
blizzard, discovered the two men. The plane managed to land near
the men and picked them up. They were suffering from frostbite,
and their rations had almost gone. The Otter plane flew on to South
Ice and landed, according to Dr. Fuchs, "in high drift, visibility of
66 yards, surface invisible."

Fuchs flew back to Shackleton and the three scientists were
left at South Ice until October, while Fuchs and his colleagues at
Shackleton prepared for the winter, overhauling gear, sledges, and
vehicles for the following Antarctic summer.

By March 1957, work was sufficiently advanced for Fuchs to
send a progress report to the London headquarters. It was as laconic
as usual, yet full of word pictures: "Depot 300 now called South
Ice. Special lightweight aluminum and plywood hut completed
February 22, together with electric light from petrol or wind gen-
erators. Hut built in five foot hole in snow to hasten drifting to
roof which ensures warmth. Temperature at South Ice already
minus 40 degrees Fahrenheit, which is 30 degrees lower than

Shackleton. So far 15 tons stores transported by air—four tons to go. Snow tunnels provide housing for stores, generator, and cold temperature laboratory."

Of Shackleton, Fuchs reported: "Exit from hut via tunnel and trapdoor at snow surface. Tunnel leads through door past bathroom, coalhouse, through workshop, then past surgery and survey office to large living room, where Queen's portrait hangs one end; other walls decorated gay travel posters and one water color. Library shelves round wall and four-berth cabins open off north wall. Ladder leads to attic store. Kitchen at east end with radio room, met office and darkroom beyond. All interior hut very warm. Each man cooks four days in rotation. Washing up, cleaning, bringing in ice for water generator, and dog feeding, etc., part-time chore for two daily.

"Breakfast 0800 hours work stops 2300 hours except for night pilot, radio operator, and met observer who rise later in the morning. Persistent wind and low temperatures coat each bearded face with rime and ice which is pulled off on entering hut revealing healthy glowing countenances. Apart from normal washing, each man in turn has bathroom for baths and clothes wash one day. Dogs still in open but going to tunnels when weather worsens. They thrive on seal meat and are now fat like woolly sheep and in good condition for winter. Recent scene at ice edge was Stratton hand-feeding killer whales who rose to steal titbits. It was reminiscent of Bertram Mills sea lions. We are hoping for balancing act by autumn. All well."

The Antarctic winter was almost there, but after their initial disasters, the camps were in good shape. The three parties—Shackleton, South Ice, and Scott Base—dug in for the long Antarctic night, concentrating on scientific work and preparing their gear. And as Bunny Fuchs casually ended his message, all was well.

When the first streaks of "dawn" heralded the end of winter, there was still one more preparatory task to be done before the expedition started. Fuchs hoped to leave early in November for the actual crossing, but prior to that, when the daylight came in October, he determined to make a proving trip to South Ice, the important steppingstone for the crossing. He planned to travel lightly, to find out the worst crevassed areas before risking all his men and machines. On October 8, he set out, while the aircraft relieved the three men who had wintered over at this lonely depot.

Fuchs found the going tremendously difficult. Though only 270 miles from Shackleton, his actual journey to South Ice covered 400 miles because of crevassed areas, and though Fuchs estimated it would take thirteen days, it took five weeks before one Sno-Cat and one Weasel and a dog team got through. One Weasel was abandoned on this reconnaissance. Almost 70 miles of the route were found to be heavily crevassed, and with the vehicles roped together, progress at times was reduced to two miles a day, and on some occasions as low as half-a-mile a day. Time after time the vehicles or dogs fell into crevasses, some of them big enough, as Fuchs said, to take a London bus. The small party plodded along the Filchner Ice Shelf and climbed the ice wall that skirted the Shackleton Mountains. All the way across the 400 miles they flagged the route, and marked the crevasses. Five weeks later they reached South Ice. Fuchs left two men there and the others flew back, leaving the Sno-Cat and the Weasel at South Ice.

These would be picked up when Fuchs returned to South Ice on the way across to the Pole. But this again was an exasperating delay; and though the *Theron* delay had been absorbed, so to speak, by the winter, this time Fuchs could not reclaim the vital time lost. The delay caused by the proving trip to South Ice was the basic reason, as Fuchs told me later, why the crossing so nearly did not succeed; he never caught up again. Yet that proving trip had to be done, for if Fuchs had not undertaken it, with the loss of only one machine, he would never have known the immense difficulties ahead and might easily have lost much more equipment on the crossing proper.

For the same reason Hillary had to test the route towards the plateau, finally deciding against climbing the Beardmore, as Amundsen and Scott had done, and choosing instead the Skelton Glacier. This was the main job of the New Zealand support force and during that Antarctic summer an advance party found an excellent route up the Skelton and reached the Polar plateau. Hillary flew up and over the plateau field party and spoke to them by walkie-talkie but could not make a landing. However, he was able to report: "We are ahead of schedule and the route appears eminently suitable to bring down the British party with their tractors and Sno-Cats."

As soon as possible after the Skelton was proved, Hillary set off to establish Depot 700—500 miles from the Pole—where Fuchs originally planned to meet him on January 10. Hillary, starting in mid-October, decided to make the journey in four stages across terrain which Scott described in his diary as "the most desolate in the world—barren, fearsomely monotonous, and piercingly cold."

"It's a job that's got to be done," said Ed Hillary, "and as soon as we've finished it, we'll all be pretty eager to get home."

Hillary set off, and was soon climbing the Skelton. At Shackleton the last preparations were made for the start of the crossing. As the weather improved, and the light started to last twenty-four hours a day, the vehicles were brought out of their garage at Shackleton base for the last time.

On the evening of November 24, nine men climbed into them and the last great journey had started. As undemonstrative as usual on this historic day, Fuchs sent a casual message back to headquarters: "Main party departed in grand style 2145 on 24 November. Three Sno-Cats, two Weasels, one Muskeg, pulling twenty tons."

There were nine men accompanying the six vehicles, with two more waiting at South Ice. The RAF supporting party of four men remained behind under John Lewis at Shackleton to give air support when needed. With them stayed Geoffrey Pratt, the seismologist and twelfth member of Fuchs' team. This decision was taken by Fuchs because of the delay in his starting time. Insistent on taking seismic soundings across the continent, Fuchs planned for Pratt to be flown by Otter to South Ice as soon as the weather permitted.

There, because of the delay, he would go ahead and do some of the seismic soundings on the route to save time after Fuchs reached South Ice.

In theory, the plan was simple. The main crossing party, which would pick up the two tracked vehicles and tons of stores already at South Ice, would average twenty miles a day across the continent. But it was going to take them four weeks before they reached South Ice, only 270 direct miles from Shackleton, and many weeks more before they reached the Pole.

Two days after the tiny party in its orange-painted vehicles set off for the murderous journey to South Ice, I entered the picture in my small way. After many months of planning, my newspaper chose me to make the journey to Antarctica to report on the expedition. I left London three days later, and thirteen days after that I was at the South Pole.

3. A Representative of the Press

THE expedition was on its way. Hillary was moving steadily forward towards Depot 700, and Fuchs, after his early disappointments, was at last on the trail and lumbering slowly towards South Ice.

Up to this time, for several reasons, the expedition had failed to capture the imagination of the British public. It was a curious fact that, despite the large number of books published in Britain about Antarctica, it was the Americans, not the British, who were the most avid readers of the dramatic opening-up of the continent. For the International Geophysical Year, Britain had very few scientists in Antarctica, compared with the Americans and the New Zealanders. The Pole was out of fashion, and even when the Americans established a base there, the attendant publicity in the United States received almost no echoes in Britain. Not one man in a hundred knew that a group of American scientists was actually living and working at the South Pole. Not one in a thousand had any real idea of what Dr. Fuchs was doing. If they knew anything about the expedition at all, it was that Hillary of Everest was in action again.

This disinterestedness was also partly due to the fact that the Trans-Antarctic Expedition had agreed to reserve its dispatches for one journal only, *The Times*, which meant that any adventure-loving reporters (or their adventure-loving editors, which is much more important) who wished to accompany the expedition would most certainly not be allowed to do so. Dr. Fuchs had signed a contract to write exclusively for *The Times*, and naturally *The Times* did not want any other newspaper represented on the expedition. Equally naturally, the rest of Fleet Street rather tended to give the expedition the cold shoulder—or rather to ignore it—for the very normal reason that any news about it was second-hand. Anyway, what was it? A lot of men trundling across a lot of ice.

For some time, though, the London *Daily Mail* had been planning to send a man to Antarctica. For several months exploratory investigations were made both in London and Washington, usually in conditions of some secrecy when possible, not only because of our rivals but because (as we had discovered with the Everest expedition) obstacles would no doubt have been put in our way by the expedition leaders. When Hillary was climbing Everest, the *Daily Mail* had pulled off a fantastic tour de force: Ralph Izzard, one of my colleagues, climbed alone to 18,000 feet chasing the expedition, only to be most improperly received when, after this great achievement, he stumbled into the camp of fellow Britons so far from home.

With this background it did not seem possible to get any member of our staff accredited to the expedition. The *Mail* had at this time, in the summer of 1957, no particular idea of their staff man going as far as the South Pole. They wanted a man in Antarctica—not too soon, for that would have been a wastage of manpower, nor too late. But where? Shackleton was out of the question. It was no good being behind Fuchs. Scott Base? Our man in New Zealand told us bluntly that, even if we managed to receive permission for a man to stay at Scott Base, all possible means would be employed to prevent him from sending dispatches on the Scott Base circuit.

So what about the Americans? It was finally decided to request Washington to accredit me to the U.S. Naval forces in Antarctica. The choice fell on me for several reasons, the most important, perhaps, being that I have twice been accredited to the United States Sixth Fleet, which was a sort of introduction to the U.S. Navy Department at the Pentagon, and I also, as a hobby, write when opportunity permits occasional magazine articles for the American *Saturday Evening Post*. I was thus able quite truthfully to say that I was a senior staff member of the *Daily Mail*, but also a *Saturday Evening Post* writer. This was a very important added lever in my request for accreditation, for the Americans naturally prefer publicity in the journals and magazines of their home country.

While the preliminary discussions with Washington were proceeding, I was somewhat busily engaged in a small but spirited war in the Oman desert, from which campaign I returned with an alarming dose of dysentery and a much reduced waistline. I took a late holiday and then about mid-November I went to London for a "Polar Conference." Up to this time no permission had been received from Washington for me to join the American forces, and their Admiral Dufek in Christchurch cabled saying that even if Washington did grant me my military orders, he, Dufek, could not guarantee me any passage to Antarctica. The weather was breaking, no icebreakers were going, and when the summer melted Antarctica's only big ice-strip there would be no more flying. This was shattering news. There was no point in going all the way to Christchurch to report the expedition from there. I went to see Commander Pillsbury, the efficient American Navy public information officer in London, who promised to press the matter, and then I myself phoned Washington to see what could be done. Not much, it seemed. I returned to my wife and family, at that moment in Paris. On Friday, November 29, the *Mail* phoned me. It was 11 A.M. No orders had come through, but they were expected hourly. What did I think? I *knew* that I would receive my orders, for I was a firm friend of many high-ranking officers, including "Cat" Brown of the Sixth Fleet.

How about planes to New Zealand?" I asked.

There was a Britannia leaving the following day.

The officer booked me a seat on this, and we decided that if my military orders did not come through, I would leave for New Zealand anyway, hoping they could be cabled after me. If I didn't get to Christchurch quickly, I would never get out to Antarctica and the whole project would be a flop.

But first I had to get to London. It was 11:15 when the conversation ended with my office in London. I ran upstairs and my wife helped me to pack tropical clothes for the New Zealand summer "in case you are stranded there." A plane was leaving Orly for London in an hour. I had just time to kiss my wife before I rushed to catch it. I little thought that exactly two weeks later I should be at the South Pole.

In London I went to see Pillsbury again, and stayed the night at the Travellers. Still no orders. Nor the next morning. I left, feeling rather worried, for London Airport, stopping to buy half a dozen books on Antarctica to read on the four-day journey to New Zealand. As a precaution, I registered my ticket in my first Christian name, John Barber. There was no point in advertising my destination. I would write nothing—not a word for the *Mail*—until my plane was ready to leave for McMurdo, so that nobody could catch me up, for if I did get a plane from Christchurch it might well be the last of the season. With just the right touch of drama, a taxi chased me to London Airport with my military orders. They had come through.

My orders from the *Mail* were simple: to report the Trans-Antarctic Expedition and any other aspects of life in Antarctica that I thought would interest its readers. There was no specific mention of the South Pole as an objective, for it was not seriously considered practicable, though Walter Farr, the Foreign Editor of the *Mail*, said wistfully what a wonderful story it would be to spend Christmas there. Nor was there any guarantee that I should ever be able to make any direct contact with either Fuchs or Hillary, already on the trail. As usual on an assignment of this sort—just as in the Budapest and Oman wars of the past twelve months—an office has to trust a man, not only with his decisions, but with large sums of money for chartering aircraft without having the time to inform the office in advance. This is—to use an American term with which I was to become familiar—"strictly routine." I have on occasion chartered a four-engine aircraft (when no smaller one was available) costing £1,000. I once chased the French troops into a battle by taxi, offering the driver £150 if he would get me there. Now again, I was on my own.

B.O.A.C. took me smoothly and silently across half the world, until the rumblings of war in Indonesia caused us some delay in Jakarta, where we had to spend several hours before permitted to proceed. I took advantage of this opportunity to stretch my legs by slipping out of the airport and seeing old friends in the capital, which I had visited before. There had been an attempt on the life of Sukarno. The city was stiff with troops. By some good fortune, this had happened the day before and no reporters had as yet been able to reach the country. I spent the time on our next hop to Perth writing a story which I filed from there, and which, in accordance with our agreement of secrecy, appeared in the next morning's *Daily Mail* without my byline.

I arrived at Christchurch on December 4, late at night, and was met at the airport by Pat Hobbs, the wife of Leslie Hobbs, the invaluable part-time *Daily Mail* man in Christchurch. A room had been reserved for me (with some difficulty) at Warner's Hotel, next to the *Press*, the leading daily newspaper for which Leslie Hobbs worked at night. Late though it was, we managed to get some sandwiches and beer and Leslie came across from the office, and we talked far into the night. Admiral Dufek, it appeared, was at McMurdo, and so was his public information officer, Commander Merle Macbain. This was a mixed blessing. It could be useful if they were still there when I arrived, but I had hoped (in my innocence) that if it were touch and go getting to Antarctica, the weight of the Admiral might swing the balance. On the other hand, once in Antarctica, the Admiral's presence at McMurdo would be invaluable.

The man to see was Captain Hawkes, and accordingly I made my number with him early the following morning. Hawkes was a legend in Antarctic flying, the first man to fly nonstop across the

Antarctic, and also in the first plane (with Admiral Dufek) ever to land at the South Pole. Hawkes, like many Americans, was invested with a nickname, in this case "Trigger," and it was said that he al-ways flew with an unlighted cigar in his mouth long before General Le May became noted for this quirk.

Dufek summed up Hawkes admirably in his book *Operation Deepfreeze* when he wrote, "Admiral Cruzen had asked me to name a squadron commander (for these aircraft). There was no hesitation on my part. It was Trigger Hawkes. Commander Hawkes showed up, cigar in mouth. I had not seen him since 1939, but the war and seven years had treated him kindly. Short, sturdy, steady, he was that rare combination—an outstanding pilot and an engineer. Given a problem he would study it, and then if it could be done, he would say, 'O.K., no strain.' There was no fear in him."

The American Navy headquarters was in a rambling building called "The Old Brewery." When I reached it, Trigger Hawkes, cigar built into the corner of his mouth like a fixture, looked me up and down.

"Here—have one. Now let's get you kitted out. You're going to be mighty cold for the next few weeks."

He looked me up and down again.

"Let's get one thing straight," he said. "You got no cold weather clothing—right? We got almost no cold weather clothing. Who pays for yours if I don't supply you?"

"Well—the *Daily Mail*, of course."

"Right. That's all I wanted to know. I don't mind sticking the *Mail* for a hundred bucks, but I didn't wanna take money off you."

Actually, the Navy fitted me out with the major items—thermo-boots, socks, thick woollen underpants, right down to the ankle like grandfather used to wear and looking very scratchy. Then layer after layer of clothes to be put on as required: thick woollen shirts, heavy pullovers, quilted trousers and a windproof quilted jacket, hats, goggles, and three pairs of gloves to be worn one on top of each other.

"That's all you'll need," said Trigger dryly. "After all, it's summer down there, you know."

With typical American swiftness, I was kitted out in less than an hour. With typical American lack of concern about equipment, I did not have to sign for anything.

"Bring it back if you don't lose it," grunted Trigger Hawkes.

"What are the chances of flying out?" I asked.

"Tomorrow," said Trigger laconically. "I'll ring you with the time. Twelve hours nonstop. You're lucky—we're sending the Admiral's plane down for him, so you'll be a V.I.P. for one night. Don't let it go to your head."

That afternoon, I bought myself some extra equipment, helped by Leslie Hobbs, who took me to the shop that equipped the Everest expedition. I stocked up with thick woollen shirts, better quality socks, pullovers, and spare sets of "waffle weave" underwear. That and a half-dozen bottles of Scotch.

I didn't leave that night, nor the next, for the head winds were too strong to warrant risking an aircraft flying over two thousand miles across Antarctic water with no place to land except the ice-strip at the destination. But on Saturday, December 7, the weather improved, and Trigger warned me to be ready to fly that night.

So at last I was to play a part, however insignificant, in this great adventure, the conquest of Antarctica. Firstly, McMurdo— and then? By skidplane, by tractor, by sled perhaps, into the white unknown, to names that were dots on maps, and not all maps at that; names like Clinker Buff, Crater Hill, Hut Point, on the great continent that contained four-fifths of the world's ice and where at that moment, Fuchs and Hillary were struggling from opposite ends to the point where eventually they would meet.

In Christchurch itself, tranquil in the early summer, with the first strawberries just coming on the market in time for Christmas, everybody was Antarctic crazy, for this was McMurdo's rearguard base. On my last night I dined with a man who had spent a year in Antarctica. Only a week before he had been knocking a stake into the hard ice when it froze to his glove with such force that he could not pull it away. Another man had to come and kick it off. It was hard to realise as I walked the trim English streets of Christ-church, with policemen still wearing old-fashioned bobbies' hats, that in a few hours I too should be winging my way to another world. It was even harder to realise that only a week previously I had been romping with my babies in front of the fire at home.

I do not know how great explorers feel at moments like this, but I do know that on that last night in Christchurch, poised on the edge of the unknown, I felt, cutting across my nostalgic longing for hearth and home, a sense of intense desire to reach ahead which I could not explain. I have always had it, but never more manifest than at that moment.

I looked back, from the lounge of Warner's Hotel, to some of the great adventures I had undertaken for the *Daily Mail*: that wonderful three-month drive from London to the Tibet border; Budapest; the wars in Morocco and Indo-China and lately in Oman; each one a lonely, yet shared, excitement. But this, I felt, would be the greatest of them all, for I did not know what would happen, nor when, nor where. But, above all, what I hoped to witness was not a sordid war of man against man, but the deeper, fundamental war of man against nature. Already man was winning the war. The Pole was inhabited. Nearly 30 aircraft had already landed there in the previous thirteen months. In the past four weeks the Americans had dropped over 700 tons of food and equipment for the men marooned there for their scientific research.

Yet it was still a war, as Hillary and Fuchs were finding out, in which, as aircraft winged overhead, men on foot might some days be lucky to travel two miles in twenty-four hours.

Was I alone in feeling like this? I found not. The bearded men in Christchurch (the beard being the hallmark of the Ant-arctic explorer) were not very communicative, for it took time to make the transition and thaw out from the lonely life, but I found that among those with whom I talked, nine out of ten ached only for the moment of return. Was this the same mystical appeal which made people like Byrd and Scott return time and again, and now had drawn Fuchs into its web?

All the hazards, and there were many, counted for nothing. All the discomforts, and there were more than many, counted for less than nothing. It was not only a sense of conquest, though how fiercely this must have been running through the veins of Fuchs and Hillary! For most men it was a more private and personal emotion.

The American with whom by chance I dined (in New Zealand hotels they have the quaint custom of allotting you seats at specific tables, regardless of whether the room is half empty) did not talk much at first, but then finally, with a heavy sigh, he looked down into his glass, and said slowly,

"Well, I guess it's this way. Life there is lousy. Hell, you don't have a bath for weeks on end. You sleep with your clothes on, you can't get a drink, you even gotta do your own laundry. And yet, dammit, I just want to get back there as fast as I can."

Perhaps that, after all, was the secret of man's passion for the White South, a love affair with an enigmatic siren who lured one on even to the edge of oblivion, but whose spell was so overwhelming that no hardship was too severe, no danger too great, for the chance of the favours that only she could bestow.

It would not be long before I found out.

4. McMurdo Camp

It was a quarter past three in the morning when I landed on the ice runway of McMurdo Sound, and the sun was shining brightly on the white world. As I clambered stiffly out of the plane, the cold hitting me like a blow between the eyes, a man with silver-grey hair came up, held out a mittened hand and said, "I'm George Dufek. Let's go and have breakfast."

So I arrived in Antarctica, 13,000 miles or so from London, little more than 800 miles from the Pole. A couple of Weasels were drawn up near the aircraft, and almost as soon as the propellors stopped turning, a maintenance crew tumbled out and started fitting covers to the engines to prevent their freezing. We stamped around on the hard snow while the baggage was unloaded and I took my first look at this different world of utterly changed values, where night and day were friends under a glaring sun that wouldn't set for at least another three months.

McMurdo Sound is not in actual fact the correct name of the camp where I had alighted. Since it was first established by the United States Navy, a succession of harassed senior officers had tried to persuade its inhabitants to call the camp by its proper, if cumbersome title, the Williams Air Operating Facility. Nobody had succeeded. To the world the camp is always McMurdo Sound, named after the strip of narrow water that curls south from the Ross Sea between Ross Island and the mainland.

I could see the huts of the camp, built on the rising ground of this small volcanic island with its ugly black patches of snowless mountainsides jutting out unromantically against the white earth around it. It wasn't very prepossessing, especially in comparison with the majestic white scene across the Sound, which reminded me irresistibly of the view from my farm across Lake Geneva. There were a couple of dozen huts, some of them salmon-colored, rough roads, an air operating center, tangled cables strung loosely between heavy poles, radio antennas, a helicopter and on the ice runway the scarlet tail-fins and wing-tips of three aircraft. As the Admiral and I made our way from the Sound up to the actual camp— a distance of nearly two miles—the snow gave way to slush and mud. It was a scene I was to know well before the great Fuchs epic was over.

On the left as we drove up was Hut Point, to which you could walk across the ice to Scott's first camp, still littered with haunches of mutton frozen for nearly fifty years, with old English magazines circa 1910, their pages stuck together. On the rising ground nearby stood the skeleton of a Globemaster that had crashed there a few months previously, enormous and grotesque, its giant aluminum fuselage looking as though it had been half eaten away by termites. Part of the wing and one engine lay in the snow and ice a quarter of a mile away. Beyond stood row after row of drums of fuel. Down the hillside lurched that ever-present phenomenon of modern Antarctica, the bulldozer, groaning pitifully on its way back from digging out snow for water, Antarctica's most precious commodity. All my time in Antarctica I never quite got used to the incessant noise of machinery day and night. McMurdo Sound at four A.M. was far noisier than Covent Garden, and just about as busy. On my right was Observation Hill, so named by Scott, and with a cross on its summit, stark against the blue sky. Round the corner, as yet unseen, was Scott Base, Sir Edmund Hillary's rear headquarters. Across the waters lay the mainland of Antarctica, while behind lay the Ross Ice Shelf, in a sense as solid as dry land—and as dry as dry land. Ross Island itself was stuck like a wart on the edge of this mighty chunk of ice up to 700 feet thick, a thousand years old, and as large as New Zealand's north island; a "country" which had gradually been formed on the sea as the ice was forced down by the glaciers behind. The cliffs on the edge of the shelf towered a hundred feet, like the white cliffs of Dover, only whiter, over the waters of the Ross Sea itself, which was unfrozen to within about ten miles of the camp. In the distance I could just see the black line of the open sea, as though somebody had drawn a thick stroke with a pencil on the edge of a white sheet.

This was to be my rear base and communications headquarters for my task of reporting the Trans-Antarctic Expedition. I do not know what I had expected, but I had never expected anything like this. A world of central heating side by side with the yelp of huskies and Antarctic clothing little changed from the days of Scott and Shackleton.

At that very moment Fuchs was fighting his way towards South Ice and Hillary was gasping his way up the Skelton Glacier—with machines, it is true, but still in the grand manner of yesterday, of men alone against nature. Yet here was I, in Antarctica also, but given a bed in a plastic hut, built on a wooden skeleton, proof against the toughest Antarctic weather, but so conceived that it could be dropped in a package complete with wooden floor and assembled ready to move in four hours.

On the trail, the expedition members were already living on pemmican and cooking two in each tent because of the cold outside, and never washing or taking off their clothes. In the hut, which I shared with three other men, I had blankets, drip oil heating, and a small metal locker for my clothes. The camp even had a small shop, with very little to sell beyond cigarettes and cases of beer, which never needed chilling if the cases were left on the cold wooden floor of the hut. One orange-colored building was the powerhouse which supplied the camp with lighting and current for communications and also had, in one corner, three washing machines and five showers, which worked out at one shower every ten days, and a turn at the washing machine once a fortnight. There were no orderlies and each man, from the Admiral down, had to wash his own clothes.

For the morning wash and cleaning your teeth, there were two square buildings, each of which contained three bowls, and three toilet seats with no privacy. One look at them decided me to wash as infrequently as possible.

Though nobody can pretend that life in Antarctica is anything but tough, a solidly established base camp can be made comparatively comfortable anywhere in the world, but comfort was the last word that could be applied to McMurdo. I had the feeling that since Antarctica was known to be rough and tough, the Americans decided to keep it that way. In a way, they enjoyed it, for the rougher it was, the less discipline there was. Though millions of dollars had been spent on establishing the base, which was stocked on a fantastic scale with equipment for scientists and fliers, there was not even one common room where the 250 men could enjoy leisure moments. There was no officers' mess. The one mess hall was also the cinema. There was a small library, but it had only two chairs. If a man wanted to read or drink a tin of beer, he had to do it sitting on his bed.

This rough and tough life applied equally to officers as well as men and, in fact, all my time in Antarctica I never saw any privileges for officers that were denied to the men except on the New Zealand vessel *Endeavour*, which had a British naval officer in command, Captain Kirkwood, known to all as Captain Plywood.

The attitude of the American officers towards their men could not have been more commendable. A great deal of it arose from the fact that Dufek, a salty character, was a man who resolutely refused any privilege in tough conditions that his men could not equally enjoy.

Dufek was, in fact, a great man, and perhaps nothing is more typical of him than this little episode which he will hate me for revealing. When a tractor team of American scientists and Navy men had been out for days on the trail, Dufek flew over by helicopter to see how they were doing. He was appalled by their dirty clothes, and immediately gathered them up, saying he would take them back to McMurdo and arrange to have them washed. But he did not arrange to have them washed. Admiral Dufek went to the powerhouse and put the clothes himself in the communal washing machine; and when they were clean, he flew back by helicopter to give his men their clothing.

I was not surprised, therefore, when the Admiral, having invited me to dine with him, did not take me to sup in the privacy of his hut, but in the canteen. There, admiral or not, Dufek had to stand in line for ten minutes until our turn came at the self-service cafeteria—where we helped ourselves to hamburgers and coffee, after which we had some difficulty in finding places among the swirling, bearded mob.

I had not, of course, travelled all the way to Antarctica to write a thesis on American naval shore establishments. I had deliberately chosen to be accredited to the U.S. Navy because experience had taught me that their press-conscious senior officers are always more likely to help newspapermen than those of the British Navy, and if I were to report the Trans-Antarctic Expedition, I would badly need help in this inhospitable continent. All the help I could get. But it took me a day or two to sort myself out, even to get used to the eternal business of putting on and taking off layers of clothes each time I stepped in or out of a hut.

Worse than that was the immediate reaction to the lack of dark in a world where you could take a photograph equally well at midday or midnight. It made no difference, the brassy sun beat down every hour of the twenty-four, giving Antarctica its only occupational disease, known as the "big eye," a local word for insomnia. Before I had been in Antarctica a week, I had already learned to sleep like an animal when nature dictated it. The incessant noise of tractors and bulldozers, the complete absence of darkness and the fact that somebody was always at work, soon made it quite impossible to know day from night. I would go to sleep, somebody would open the door of the hut and a shaft of almost unbearable sunlight made me think I had overslept even at two in the morning. On my first night I didn't go to bed at all. Around eight A.M., feeling slightly debauched, I turned in. At eleven somebody woke me up by mistake, so I dressed and went to meet the various officers of the camp. At six P.M., feeling sleepy, I went back to bed. I awoke at ten P.M., and stayed up until three in the morning.

"It doesn't make any difference," Dufek said, "when the 'big eye' is watching you."

It didn't. But at least the "big eye" gave me the time to explore the fringes of this strange continent that has gripped so many men. Helicopters flew me round Mount Erebus or along the edge of the Shelf. There was always a Navy Otter plane to take me further inland to savour the mystical magic that belongs to Antarctica alone.

Now that I am home, and with a shelf of books on Antarctica by my side, I cannot bring myself to describe in words that could only be plagiarism, my thoughts and ambitions as I started to probe the white continent. I had become a member of Operation Deepfreeze, and as *Time* magazine said:

"The men of Operation Deepfreeze found the continent a harsh, hauntingly beautiful and, above all, strange land. The snow crystals that drift down over its great central plateau seem dry as sand. Yet, because there is little ablation—return of moisture to the atmosphere—this light precipitation has become a glacier of up to a mile or more in depth. Under its own weight the ice moves glacially, spilling down off the plateau, flowing imperceptibly but inexorably towards the sea, squeezing through valleys, crawling over hills, plunging down the sides of mountains in great frozen cataracts. What it does not bury or crush, it encircles. And finally, at the continent's rim, it meets the frozen seas, and ice battles ice on a titanic scale. Vast crevasses shudder open along the tortured ridges; ice

rafts as large as the state of Connecticut are torn loose from the continental shelf and set floating like derelict monsters in the frigid
waters."

In this eerie and strange world, into which I had been so
swiftly plunged, my first task was to find out the latest progress of
the expedition, and for this I trekked across to Scott Base. Though
only two miles from McMurdo, through a pass under the lee of
Observation Hill, it was a different world. Gone were the ugly black
stains of volcanic ash that smeared the hillsides at McMurdo, gone
was the slush and the mud. Protected by the mountains, Scott Base
was always clothed in white. It took me forty minutes to walk
there, after having signed out at the Administration Building of
McMurdo, a formality insisted upon when anybody left camp, in
case of sudden "whiteouts."

Scott Base was much smaller, with fewer than a couple of dozen
men. At the foot of the base, a cluster of bright yellow huts, an
Otter, and a Beaver aircraft were moored. The New Zealand flag
fluttered over the main hut, which was linked to the others by tunnels, and the officer in charge was Squadron Leader John Claydon,
of the New Zealand Royal Air Force. I took an instant liking to
him. He was intelligent, forthright, and always prepared to offer
sound advice on the latest plans of Fuchs and Hillary. He invited
me in for a cup of tea. The combined living room and dining room
had small tables, a kitchen near by, and a kettle on the hob, so that
anybody at Scott could always make tea or coffee when he wished,
in direct contrast to the larger mess hall of McMurdo, where you
had to take your food and drink at regulated hours. The room was
warm and cosy, and Claydon and I lolled back in armchairs and
talked things over.

Scott Base had its post office from which a New Zealand journalist, seconded to *The Times* for the expedition, was able to send
out messages, but though this was in actual fact a post office with
its own stamps and postmaster (Hillary), it was not possible for me
to use this for journalistic purposes. It had been established for the
use of *The Times* and that was all there was to it. The position

with this post office was always a little confused. I was always at liberty to telephone to New Zealand or post letters from it, or send private cables to my wife. But it was hinted that any "commercial" cables would be held back through "pressure of other work." And it was certainly true that the small radio station was overworked with expedition cables. However, the fact that I could use the telephone for private conversations was of the utmost importance. My problem would always be to get out important news—of Fuchs and Hillary meeting, or of an accident, or anything of interest to the British readers—at least as quickly as *The Times*, though preferably before them. McMurdo had already warned me that though the naval authorities would do everything to help me, there would at times be serious delays. So I devised a code to be telephoned from Scott Base to my contact in New Zealand in case of emergency.

This was Leslie Hobbs, whose wife had met me when I arrived in Christchurch. But I could never have telephoned Leslie from Scott Base directly in a moment of crisis. I would just never have got through. So I decided I would telephone Pat, his wife, instead. When the plane that had brought me to McMurdo returned to Christchurch, it carried a letter in which I had written out a whole series of phrases relating to an alleged romance between Pat and myself. Each phrase meant something entirely different. For example, if I asked her "Do you love me?" it meant "Fuchs has lost a vehicle in a crevasse." Every phrase of import was in the form of a question, so that in ordinary conversation Pat did not have to worry. But as soon as I said to her, "Darling, I have a question to ask you," she would have her pencil at the ready and keep her eye on the list of questions stuck up on the wall in front of the telephone at her house. These had numbers against them, so all she had to do was write down a number. Once I had finished talking, her husband would pick up the telephone again and give the "flash" to London.

In actual fact I was able to get most of my news out of McMurdo, but the problem was—getting the news. McMurdo had no real interest in the Fuchs expedition and so no news about it was available there. John Claydon told me that he received almost daily reports at Scott Base from Fuchs and Hillary, but though he promised to give me as many details as possible, it was going to be rather a hit and miss affair. Even the freakish weather would make it quite impossible for me, on occasion, to walk from McMurdo to Scott. Claydon was perfectly willing to help if he could, and in fact was very much opposed to the policy of giving the news to one journal only, though I must admit I could understand *The Times* wishing to protect its investment. I had no quarrel with *The Times*, I was only interested in finding a way round the difficulty.

The clue came in casual conversation with John Claydon. I asked him, almost without thinking, "Isn't it amazing that Fuchs has a radio strong enough to reach all the way to Scott Base?"

"Good God"—John poured out another cup of tea—"he can't possibly make direct contact with us. He gives a daily message to the Americans at the South Pole. They then send it on to us. We send our messages to Fuchs via the Pole too. The Americans have been damned decent—they've given us every facility. They talk to Fuchs every day. We use the Pole as a sort of relay station."

Immediately, of course, this put an entirely different aspect on everything. Even if it had been possible to speak to Fuchs from Scott Base, I do not think I should have been allowed to. The post office at Scott Base had its very clear terms of reference, and they did not include services to the press. But supposing I could get up to the South Pole? Everything would be changed. The South Pole was an American Navy station, and I knew from my service with the U.S. Sixth Fleet that the U.S. Navy invariably makes all messages except those classified for military secrecy available to the press. Even better, from the informality of the Pole, I might even be able to talk to the Fuchs expedition myself. Why not?

Of course, there was one snag—getting there. Looking back now, I can remember as though it were only yesterday, trudging back across the ice to McMurdo, my brain buzzing with excitement, and wondering how best to persuade Admiral Dufek to get me to the Pole if it were humanly possible. Until that moment, I had never seriously considered the South Pole as a major objective of my assignment. There had been jokes in the office about what a good story it would be to spend Christmas at the Pole, but my assignment was to report the Fuchs story before anything else. A biting wind stung my face as I walked through the pass and the brown and white patchwork quilt of McMurdo came into view on the other side. I pulled the fur hood of my parka tighter round my chin. Why not? I still, most certainly, didn't realise the significance of visiting the South Pole, nor the stir that this story within a story would make a few days later. I saw one thing only—a chance to talk to members of the Fuchs expedition and, as a change from the factual and laconic reports in *The Times*, to give British newspaper readers some idea of what life was like with Fuchs on the trail towards South Ice.

I was diffident about approaching the Admiral. There was the question of protocol. Dufek had a public information officer, Merle Macbain ("mac and a small b," he grunted the first time I met him). Merle, like all the Americans of senior rank, was a grand fellow, but he had already warned me that three American journalists were hoping to fly to the Pole at Christmas, and there would probably be no flights before then. But I wanted to go now—the next day—if I could.

As it happened, the whole problem solved itself. The following morning, Dufek and I were queueing up for lunch when he said, "Noel—what say you and I take a helicopter out to see some penguins?"

We did—that afternoon. We flew past the lazy, smoking volcano of Mount Erebus, landed on the other side of Ross Island at a penguin rookery, and spent three hours on a sunny afternoon watching the antics of the world's best-dressed birds. Long before we flew back, it was all arranged. The Navy had been considering sending up a plane on a special flight to the Pole with some urgently needed supplies and a dentist. Now they had an added person. "All right," said Dufek, "if you really want to go we'll try and get you off tomorrow," adding, "It's a tough trip and you're lucky—there probably won't be another plane going up to the Pole for nearly a month."

A lot of varying opinions have been voiced about the "milk run" to the Pole. It would ill become me to suggest that it was a mission of the most hazardous nature, but it would be silly not to point out that flying to the South Pole is not, as yet, the sort of trip which the average housewife would accept jubilantly as first prize in a competition. As Dufek wrote in his book *Operation Deepfreeze*, the ice-covered continent of Antarctica has the worst flying weather in the world. Its dangers are obvious—as obvious as the dangers of children crossing the street. There are always dangers in flying, but if you develop engine trouble in a big modern aircraft, you have three more motors to carry you along, you have alternative airfields for emergency landings, you have, above all, radio communication and modern aids like radar and weather data. Almost all this is lacking in polar flights and, above all, most of the aircraft are old. The plane in which I was to fly was a DC3, seventeen years old, and equipped with skis. And once aloft there was always the possibility (as I was to see for myself more than once) that both the point of departure and arrival would be completely hidden by whiteouts.

This question of Antarctic weather is the one factor which is most difficult to explain to people who cannot imagine its sudden bursts of savagery, nor its effect on machines (more than men) when the temperature is lower than minus fifty degrees.

The afternoon that Dufek and I went penguin hunting was perfect, but that night a wind tore across the camp so fiercely you could hardly walk from one hut to another. All expeditions to places like Scott Base were banned. Only the week before, a blizzard had sprung up on a calm day, risen to 55 miles an hour, and in a matter of seconds had twisted one Globemaster round eighty degrees. But even the blizzards were nothing compared with the dreaded whiteouts in which a man could get lost in three minutes in what looked like perfect weather.

The whiteouts started up in clear weather when the sun was

reflected between the snow and a flat-bottomed cloud. The snow reflected the sunlight back to the cloud, which in turn bounced it downwards again. The result was one of the most frightening experiences I have ever known. It was like being submerged in a pool of milk. Every semblance of horizon vanished, and if you did not want to fall off a ledge of ice or into a crevasse in a world that had no horizon, there was only one thing to do, as Fuchs and Hillary had to do time and time again. This was to take some dark object, such as a pipe or a fountain pen, throw it a few feet ahead, walk towards it, pick it up, then throw it again. Otherwise no man could tell where his world ended in a whiteout. We had serious crashes, mainly of helicopters, due to whiteout condition. One pilot was caught in a whiteout at low altitude and had no idea of his height, so he threw his pen out of the side of the helicopter to watch it fall. But it didn't fall. It stayed parallel to the aircraft. He was hovering three feet from an iceberg and could not see it.

Pilots flying Globemasters into McMurdo were always complaining of the impossibility of accurately measuring their height above ground when landing. The Navy had tried to make snowbanks at each side of the runway, but they were invisible. Finally, the Air Force Globemaster pilots brought along a supply of Christmas trees each ten feet high. These were planted at each end of the runway, and though they soon withered, they were still able to give the pilots an indication of height during landing and take-off.

The Navy, used to carrier landings, were derisive about these safety measures on the part of the Air Force, and planted a sardonic sign by the end of the runway, which read, "Army Troop Carrier Squadron. Quiet, Pine Trees Growing." But those pine trees played an important part in keeping the air accidents down.

Already two Globemasters and two helicopters had crashed. So had an Otter, while the ancient Dakotas were being forced down on the ice regularly. In my three months in Antarctica, I was four times involved in forced landings, though luckily with no dire results. Almost always it was the weather that let us down, switching at a moment's notice from the meteorological forecast into storm

or whiteout conditions. The pilots at McMurdo never really liked
the flight to the Pole. Gus Shinn, the first man ever to land a plane
at the South Pole used to say, "You just fly straight up to the Beardmore Glacier and bear right!" but I noticed that when he had a
Pole flight on his hands he attended personally to every detail of
the preflight arrangements.

Gus was one of the greatest pilots with whom I have ever flown.
Young, tough, with his hair closely cropped in a crewcut, he nursed
his ancient Dakota with the attention of a mother to her baby. She
was almost held together with bits of string and wires and she
rattled like an old tin can, but her engines purred sweetly on even
the coldest days and she never let us down. *Que Sera Sera* was the
name painted on the nose of the aircraft, but she had an even more
familiar nickname, painted on the inside of the door—The Old
Charger—and she had one added attraction which didn't exist in
the other aircraft making the South Pole flight—a few bucket seats
along one side; not the most comfortable in the world, but at least
seats. On every other flight to the Pole, I had to sit on the floor of
the aircraft that was carrying me there and back.

So it was arranged. But then the next day the weather clamped
down; we could not even see the airstrip from the camp. The whole
of the Sound was blotted out. Even so, I sent off a long cable to the
Daily Mail, giving them some of my first impressions of McMurdo,
and acquainting them with the fact that I hoped at a moment's
notice to leave for the South Pole in search of my proper assignment, to find out how Fuchs was getting on.

All that day—it was Thursday, December 12—the weather
prevented all flying. I hung around the camp wondering how long
it would last.

"Could keep up like this for a week," Merle Macbain looked
up from the book of chess problems he was studying, "but you don't
have to worry. Just relax. Each day's the same as all the others. Here
—have a ginger ale!"

This was a joke, for excellent tinned ginger ale was free at Mc-
Murdo. An enormous quantity had been brought in by ship, but

the freezing had forced the lids of the cans to bulge so that they could not be opened by an ordinary tin-opener, the sort that pierces two holes in a can of beer. Immediately the sale dropped to zero— for nobody at McMurdo would pay for the privilege of doing extra work. In the end the stocks were given gratefully to anybody who would take "the damned tins away," as the supply officer said. I never drank so much ginger ale in my life.

After struggling through two tins (ginger ale doesn't taste the same without whisky) I went to bed early, very tired with the excitement. Just in case the weather lifted, I laid out all my heavy equipment on the floor by the side of my cot. It was an absolute flying rule that all men going to the Pole had to take complete survival gear, including extra changes of all clothing in case of being stranded there or being forced down on the Polar Cap. And since day and night were the same, Shinn would take off for the Pole irrespective of the hour, as soon as the weather cleared.

At four-thirty the next morning, the door of the hut was opened, and as the sunlight streaked through, somebody shook me and asked,

"You Barber? You are? Better get yourself a cuppa coffee. You leave in an hour."

It was an utterly beautiful morning and I was ready in ten minutes. Three-quarters of an hour later, the motors of the *Que Sera Sera* started to turn and the Old Charger began to shake and quiver and snort. Her skis were stuck to the ice, but Gus Shinn managed to shake them loose. We lurched out to the end of the ice-strip, with the dentist and myself sitting in the back. A couple of minutes later we were airborne. I was on my way to the Pole. It was Friday the thirteenth of December.

5. South Pole Base

As the rhythm of the Old Charger settled down into a steady beat, and we flew across the Ross Ice Shelf, I started to read the notes I had made of the meager information available about the progress of Fuchs and Hillary. As always in those comparatively early days of the expedition, it was good news about Hillary and bad about Fuchs.

Hillary was, on this day, 60 miles from a point in the middle of nowhere called Depot 700—700 miles from Scott Base, 500 miles from the South Pole. His two dog teams had raced sixty miles ahead and were at the actual site of the depot. Hillary was chasing them with his light Ferguson tractors, though he had lost his only Weasel. I do not think Hillary ever minded abandoning the Weasel. He was in love with his Fergusons, vehicles originally intended for base work and only used for this journey on the adventurous insistence of Hillary. Depot 700 was on the plateau where Hillary's main task was to establish the base with the aid of John Claydon, who would fly up supplies from Scott in the Beaver or Otter. It was never intended that Hillary should go to the South Pole, but neither was it ever intended that he should

stand fast at 700 to await Fuchs. Hillary's task was to establish
a base, and then *either* remain there and await Fuchs if he were
expected soon or, if he so desired, return to Scott Base, ready to
fly back to 700 at the right moment. Fuchs would have been the
last man in the world to suggest to Hillary that he should sit out on
the ice at 700 indefinitely. Originally it had been hoped that Hillary
would establish 700 just as Fuchs pushed over the Polar Cap towards
this imaginary point on the map, but that was not to happen, for
as Hillary reached 700, Fuchs, nearly 1,200 miles away on the other
side of the continent, was in sore trouble.

For two days there had been no news of him, as his team of
twelve men and their seven battered vehicles, severely punished by
crevasses, crawled up a treacherous 20-mile ice wall which barred
their way to South Ice. It was at the foot of this very same wall that
Fuchs, during his reconnaissance of the route in October, had had
to abandon one of his vehicles. Now he was being held up by it
again, and already he was a long, long way behind his schedule. As
I flew up towards the Pole, Fuchs was attempting to pull up the one-
in-ten gradient of the ice wall loads of as much as eight tons
apiece.

At the moment this was all I knew, and I had cabled the gist
of it to London; while waiting for the Old Charger to warm up, I
had also typed out a hundred words or so to be sent off from Mc-
Murdo as soon as I was airborne. Due to the twelve hours difference
in time (McMurdo and Scott being on New Zealand time, twelve
hours ahead of London) this dispatch should have reached London
in time for Thursday night's paper, but it never got there, and the
only news my editor had of my movements was an earlier message
indicating that, weather permitting, I hoped to fly to the Pole on
the Friday. After that a complete silence which, in the best tradition of Fleet Street, gave my newspaper an excellent opportunity to
pose, with some drama, the question to our readers, "Is Barber at
the Pole?"

I fear that, though this volume is concerned mainly with the
fortunes of the Trans-Antarctic Expedition, as I saw it unfold, this

chapter in a way must belong to me. It is not that I wish to claim undue credit for an air journey to the Pole which was on the "milk run" but, purely as a result of my professional duties, I did in fact reach the South Pole before any of the expedition members, and so it seems to me that this is the time to describe in detail this small man-made oasis which was in turn visited by Hillary and Fuchs, with myself on each occasion waiting there to greet them. Nobody but an idiot would compare the rigours of my eight-hour journey to the Pole with the magnificent determination that Fuchs and Hillary were displaying on the trail. All I will say about my share in the adventure is that I was very excited to be flying up for the first time, and I liked it less the second and the third visits I made. But I am a newspaperman, and any journalist who has ink in his veins will never even think consciously of any discomfort if the goal is worth while. As far as I personally was concerned, Fate plus first-rate staff work by my office had placed me in an enviable position which I would never have believed possible in this modern world. It had given me the opportunity of being the first Britisher to reach the South Pole since Scott; but it had done more than that. An exclusive story for a couple of days is one thing, but on this occasion (though I was not to know it yet) Fate and bad weather decreed that my exclusive dispatches from the Pole about the expedition should continue not for hours or days, but literally for weeks. Here I was in Antarctica, the only British journalist. As soon as my first Pole story was printed, the rush started. Rivals started descending on the U.S. Navy authorities demanding permission to fly in. But there was nothing that anybody could do about it. A wall of filthy weather kept every other journalist out of Antarctica for weeks, even through Christmas, even through Hillary's arrival at the Pole. It was a fantastic state of affairs, and I cannot imagine any other part of the world where it could happen. No, this was no time to worry about the hazards of flying. There was a job to be done—solo, too.

The Old Charger droned across the Shelf towards the foot of the Beardmore Glacier. It was very cold, for there was almost no heating in the aircraft, but the weather was clear. After an hour or so, Gus Shinn came back and one of the crew members brought cardboard cartons of hot soup and some old toast and peanut butter —breakfast. The cabin of the aircraft was filled with cargo, excepting amidships where an enormous gasoline tank, rather like the boiler of a locomotive, had been installed. This gave Gus nearly 400 extra gallons of gasoline—a lot for a twin-engined aircraft— but the presence of all this petrol so near at hand did not, fortunately, prevent anybody from smoking.

I imagined we would make the Pole in one hop, but around seven in the morning we started to descend.

"I want to stop at Liv Station," said Gus. "If you're as cold as I am, you'll want a cup of coffee as much as I do."

Liv Station had all the crazy fantasy one would expect when Americans decide to open up a continent, for it was nothing more nor less than a gasoline filling station. Situated about 300 miles from McMurdo, it consisted of two plastic huts, inhabited by three men (who would eventually spend the seven-month Antarctic winter there), and a supply of airplane fuel. It was quite ridiculous, but Gus explained that with the DC3, the climb up the Beardmore to the Polar Cap took a lot of extra fuel, and because of the treacherous weather and ever-present possibility of forced landings, he hated to overload his plane with gasoline anyway.

"Going up I like to stop at Liv," he added, "but when we come back, it's downhill all the way, so we should be able to make it in one go."

Gus brought his plane down beautifully on the raw ice, and then roared across the terrain towards the two little huts with all the verve of a French taxi driver.

"Gotta keep her going," he yelled, "otherwise the skis'll stick in the snow."

The three men came racing out to meet us from the loneliest inhabited place in the world. Liv, like McMurdo, was wrongly named, and if you see it on one of the few maps, such as the National Geographic map of Antarctica, that mark it, it will be found at the foot of the Liv Glacier. This was where the Americans first established the tiny base, but later, for convenience, they moved it, lock, stock, and gasoline dump, to the foot of the Beardmore. The name stayed.

We kept the motors running even during refuelling, and the crew and dentist and I stamped across the ice to the hut where the men lived, worked, and slept, the other hut being for stores. They had a huskie with them, a few tattered books, a radio set, of course, for contacting McMurdo, and an iron stove in the center of the hut on which a pot of coffee bubbled. There was no formality at Liv, just because Gus Shinn was a lieutenant commander. Nor did it matter that the cups were not of the cleanest; the coffee could not have tasted better.

I thought, frankly, that the three men were all slightly crazy, as I would certainly have been, left alone in that white wilderness. Of the three, one hardly spoke a word all the hour we were there. The second had hair almost down to his shoulders, but was clean shaven, remarking with an irony that he didn't quite realize, "I hate people who don't shave. So dirty." This might have been directed at the third member of the party who had an enormous beard, and who, when asked how they passed the time, muttered, "We used to play cards until the dog ate the seven of spades."

Just as we were going out to the airplane again, the silent man spoke. Gus asked him a direct question—"Looking forward to being relieved and going back to McMurdo?"

The man's eyes gleamed. "Sure am," he said, "I sure love Mc-Murdo."

"More than I do," grunted the dentist. "What the hell you see in McMudhole?"

"It's the seals," said the man, "I like to go down and kill the seals."

It was time to get airborne!

From Liv we started to climb as we passed through one of the world's most awe-inspiring sights, the Beardmore Glacier. I think I can say that, in all my travels, I have never seen a sight that stunned me so much with its sheer beauty. It was up the treacherous Beardmore that Scott and his four companions made their tragic journey in 1911–12, which ended in their deaths on their way back from the Pole. Shackleton, too, had climbed this natural stairway, over a hundred miles long, with its gaping crevasses and frozen cascades, only to turn back 112 miles short of the Pole. Now it was not only a place of exquisite beauty, but an old friend to the Polar pilots, marking their flight path through the Queen Maud range of mountains from the end of the Ross Ice Shelf to the plateau.

Underneath, as we climbed, the glacier twisted and turned like a broad, majestic river, flanked on either side by great ranges and peaks. The ice was sometimes so blue I was tempted to believe that indeed it was a river. At times it was narrow, at others, thirty miles across. The peaks above it were brown, white and blue. Tributary glaciers from the Polar Cap came in like veins of a leaf, all moving relentlessly down towards the Ross Sea, where for time beyond count these great ice rivers have flooded into the sea and so formed the Ice Shelf.

Gus took the Old Charger round the corners as though piloting a ship, but soon the weather started to change. As we climbed to the top of the glacier, heavy cloud blotted everything out. Only our radar, with its yellow blobbing finger, warned us of neighbouring peaks. The winds increased, for ice is not the only thing that flows down the Beardmore and its neighboring ice canyons. The cold, heavy air from the Polar plateau always thrusts and seeks its ways downwards, and so is channelled into the natural chasms of the glaciers.

"May have to turn back," said Gus, "looks as though the weather is really closing in."

In this part of the world there was virtually no really good weather data. The Pole broadcast a daily weather forecast, but it could alter so quickly and radio communication was so bad, that all could be changed, and the pilot know nothing about it, in a matter of minutes. We tried to reach the Pole station on our radio but couldn't.

"Trouble is, you can't tell," explained Shinn. "Might be beautiful at the Pole. Only thing to do is go up and see for ourselves."

By the time we reached the top of the Beardmore, at 12,000 feet, it began to get very cold. Even my mukluks couldn't keep my feet warm. Below we could see nothing, except an occasional glimpse of the snow and ice, but even then I was never certain whether it was snow or cloud.

When we reached the Pole, I saw it for a second, marked by a circle of old oil drums, then it vanished. It didn't look more than a hundred feet below us. (Actually, Gus was flying 200 feet above ground level.) Then a whiteout came down. I saw the Pole station, the black smudge of half-buried huts, then that vanished too. It took Gus Shinn three tries to land the Old Charger because, more than any other air station in Antarctica, he had to be desperately careful at the Pole to land on the actual air strip. This was because the heavy program of air drops had left many crevasses, one of them 45 feet deep, where a tractor slipped its bearings while being parachuted down. At Liv, Gus landed quite happily on the raw ice, but at the Pole such a thing was inconceivable. The air strip was marked by a single line of barrels along one side, and the end was distinguished by strips of scarlet day-glow material. But even at two hundred feet it was impossible to see it for the first three passes.

"I'll give it one more go," said Gus, "but if we don't make it this time, we've got to go back to Liv."

There was nobody to help him. The Pole station did not have any experienced ground-to-air staff capable of leading a plane in. Gus was on his own. We circled round at low altitude, and then came down. And this time we made it, and the Old Charger landed as comfortably as a Britannia at London airport. A few moments later I wrenched open the aircraft door and jumped out and I was at the Pole.

This was going to be the spot on earth where first Hillary then Fuchs would arrive in triumph. It was going to be, and very soon too, the center of a violent argument between the factions who approved or otherwise of Hillary's dash to the Pole. Even I had no inkling that I would be flying up there twice more and, even as I landed, I did not know that I should stay four days on this, my first trip. I expected to stay for a bite of lunch, try and contact Fuchs, and then (as I had to go when the airplane went) fly straight back to McMurdo.

In worsening weather, I walked across the ice to the collection of huts peeping out of the snow where eighteen men—nine Navy men, nine scientists—lived at the bottom of the world, for a year at a time, perhaps at once the most exciting and the most boring assignment open to man.

With Gus and the two leaders of the Pole station, I ducked under a tunnel of snow and entered the main living-room of the camp. There we all started to take off layers of heavy clothing and dump them in a corner. The main hut had tubular lighting—that was the first thing that struck me—and aluminum walls. On one wall was a big blackboard tracing temperatures. I noticed one figure minus 102 degrees. The room was warm and comfortable and spotlessly clean as we sat down for the inevitable cup of navy coffee. Along one side were five tables placed end to end with chairs or benches for eating or writing. That—with a long-playing gramophone at the end—took up half of the rectangular room. Alongside, for a quarter of the room, was the galley with its hot stove and coffee pots. The most conspicuous thing there was a large block of snow from which the cook cut off a slice every time he needed water for the coffee-pot. Two modern electric toasters kept company with this primitive water supply. The other quarter of the hut was the recreation section. The gramophone was playing Mendelssohn as I walked in. Books and magazines lined the walls, and on a small bench was the "Pole Post Office" which cancelled American stamps with its magical dateline, so sought after by philatelists.

Other huts radiated from this. There was a small radio shack, sleeping quarters, science rooms, a combined bathroom, toilet and washhouse with its inevitable washing machine and electric razor plug. There was a garage for two Weasels and two tractors, and in one corner of it a snow melter. All these huts were linked by tunnels covered with six feet of snow for insulation, the corridors being used for food and fuel storage—enough food for five years, enough fuel for three. Altogether the station had 1,300 feet of tunneling, some going deep into the snow for scientific work in winter, others broadening out for the crates of food and stacks of spare scientific machines.

Two men ran the station—Lieutenant Vernon Houk, the Navy boss, a doctor and only twenty-seven, and Palle Morgenson, "Mogy" to everybody, a Danish-American, who was in charge of the important scientific work. Both were as eager to show me around as house-proud newlyweds, for these eighteen men were genuinely and delightfully excited at the state of their station.

Little more than a year before, no man had lived there. Then Dufek had landed, and the predecessors of Vern and Mogy had spent the first twelve months there building the station out of its parachuted supplies.

The buildings were prefabricated, aluminum on the inside, a layer of fiber-glass insulation, and plywood on the outside. These buildings, dropped by parachute, could withstand temperatures of 100 degrees below zero, and winds of a hundred miles an hour. Cargo after cargo of food had been dropped by Globemaster and stacked neatly away by the men of the camp. It was, I found, infinitely better than the food at McMurdo (probably because cooking for a small number of men invariably means better quality). I know that all the time I was there I ate like a horse, yet still lost weight. The usual ratio for a U.S. Navy man is about 3,200 calories, but at the Pole the men averaged 5,200 calories a day. Each man was hand-picked—as he had to be to spend a winter at the Pole.

Dufek told me that when it was decided to establish a Pole station, the first screening of the men began with the records of the volunteers. Each man had to pass a physical examination equivalent to that of "qualified for submarine duty."

"In our atomic submarines," added Dufek, "it isn't the fuel or mechanical equipment that limits the time out on patrol, but rather the limit of human endurance. The situation is comparable at places like the Pole. During the winter night, with total darkness and the temperature plunged to seventy or eighty degrees below zero, men have to live in close quarters. That is when tempers grow short and nerves are strained."

During the Antarctic winter it was often quite impossible to go outside for days at a time, so at the Pole, snow for water was obtained from a mine that went down underneath the huts in which the men lived. This in itself was a fantastic achievement in such a climate, for it descended ninety feet below the surface with steps to successive platforms that looked eerily blue as I started to walk down. In fact the ice in the mine was so blue it was the only place at the Pole where one didn't need antiwhite glasses. In the mine, men sawed snow with ordinary handsaws, cutting it into blocks that were loaded on sleds and drawn to the surface, in one of the tunnels, by tractor winch. It was the toughest job at the South Pole, for the temperature in the snow mine was never higher than sixty degrees below zero. Each man had to work a minimum of two hours a week in the mine to keep the camp in water, while the glaciologists who used the mine to study ice at depth went down every day.

It was quite obvious that there would be no flying for some time.

"Better decide now to get your bags in," said Vernon, so Gus, the crew members, and myself were given cots and sleeping bags in a plastic hut slightly apart from the main camp. This was the emergency hut, to be used in case fire wiped out the main camp— always a grave danger because of the lack of water. This hut, which soon came to be nicknamed the South Pole Press Club, was almost covered with snow, and had stacked around it, covered with parachute silk, enough food and fuel for six months, together with cots and bags for the whole station. It would have been rough living in it through an Antarctic winter, but it would have been possible.

The Press Club, however, was not linked by tunnel to the main camp, which meant that, though it only took two minutes to walk there, I had to dress up to the eyes, literally, to make the hundred yards or so. It wasn't only the reading on the thermometer that made one cold; it was the combination of temperature and wind force. On one beautiful windless day at the Pole, I stripped to the waist for sun-bathing at minus ten degrees. But on another day, clothed in layer after layer of heavy material, I nearly got frostbite at minus five—because of the sharp wind.

Dufek summed it up: "Wind reduces the temperature acting on the body about one degree for a force of each knot. Thus, in a temperature of twenty degrees below, with a wind blowing twenty knots, the temperature acting on the body would be forty degrees below zero."

I found myself desperately cold on the first day, partly because of the wind, partly because of the altitude, and when I made the pilgrimage to the actual site of the Pole, unromantically ringed by oil drums, half a mile from the camp, I wore just about every stitch of clothing I possessed—three pairs of socks under my mukluks, long pants, padded trousers, thick vest, flannel shirt, heavy pullover, two scarves, then padded coat incorporating windbreaker. I had a navy-type hat with earflaps, and over that my windproof hood with fur trimmings and straps across the chin. Finally, three pairs of gloves—one nylon, one wool, the third an enormous outer case of mittens, easy to slip on and off and slung around my neck so they wouldn't get lost.

As I trudged across the ice—the ice that stretched out 500 miles or more in every direction from the point where I stood—I wondered how Fuchs and Hillary were getting on. The utter desolation of the scene was almost frightening. For hundreds of miles, whichever way one turned, not a beast nor a bird lived, not a blade of grass grew. It was the pivot point of a savage, tyrannical continent that gave no quarter, but here, at least, it had been tamed by the Americans.

At the Pole itself the American flag was flying in a stiff breeze, but that night I planted the Union Jack by its side, the first time it had flown there since Scott was at the Pole. It was not the best British flag in the world, for I painted it on a large white handkerchief, but it had to do. That night, too, in broad "daylight" of course, Vern spent three hours digging a hole in the hard ice for a man-sized flagstaff and the following morning, at a brief ceremony, the blue and white flag of the United Nations was hoisted side by side with the Stars and Stripes. It has never been taken down to this day.

I was naturally eager to make the quickest possible contact with Fuchs, but there was no possibility on the first day. Fuchs had a radio schedule with the Pole each morning at ten. Sometimes it was possible to talk on voice frequencies, at other times the static was so bad the message had to be tapped out in Morse. The radio shack at the Pole was tiny, but it was very efficiently run by two men, so that there was always a man on duty. They took down any messages that Fuchs wanted passed on, then had an afternoon schedule with Scott Base or Hillary on the trail (if they could get a contact with him) giving them the latest news from Fuchs, and then taking any messages that would be transmitted to Fuchs the following morning. This was how Fuchs and Hillary kept in touch. Naturally, the messages were brief. Normally they included the exact position of each branch of the expedition, and this in itself would be of the utmost value to me, for I could then work out on a map the distances covered since previously reported positions and get some idea of the pace Fuchs was making. But there was nothing to be done that first day—except to wander in a slight daze round and round the camp, absorbing the fascinating details of this strange new world.

The privacy, for example. At McMurdo there was no privacy, though I later tried to make myself a cubicle with army blankets strung on rope near my cot. At the Pole, the eighteen members of the station had the same basic facilities as those at McMurdo—a hut, a bed, some blankets. Yet each man had built up round his bed space fantastic little private worlds, which indirectly reflected the characters of the men. Vernon Houk had his bed and a tiny desk made out of a packing case. He had built a wall of plywood round it, with a curtain door of parachute silk. An obvious intellectual who appreciated the better things of life, he had painted above his bed two small imitation windows, and decorated them with home-made curtains of blue and scarlet parachute silk. From old pieces of painted cardboard he had cut out vivid artificial flowers.

Mogy on the other hand liked more bed space, but instead of a desk had made an armchair where he could relax. Out of old butter boxes he had made bookshelves round the bed, with books in English and Danish and photographs of his family ranged on the top shelf. He, too, had built himself a wall of wood. Others merely curtained their spaces off from the next bed with the ever-present gaily coloured silks from parachutes that lay dotted all over the immediate white vicinity of the camp, waiting to be picked up. As always with the Americans, the "extras" such as packing cases, old parachutes, empty drums, were never recovered for possible future use. Once a parachute had served its purpose at the Pole it was thrown away—or left, a bright splash of color, on the snow.

The food was far better too. In fact, by and large, it was very good indeed, considering all the problems, and much more civilized meal hours were kept than at McMurdo. And as at Scott Base, you could walk into the galley any time you liked and cut yourself a slice of bread and jam or pour yourself a cup of coffee. At McMurdo, this was naturally not possible because of the size of the operation. At the Pole, Sunday was "brunch" day to give the cook a few hours of liberty. We got up when we liked, and cooked our own combined breakfast and lunch of bacon and powdered eggs, sausages, fried bread. That had to last us through the day until the big meal at six P.M., which was cooked professionally. Each man on the station, including Vernon and Mogy, took turns to be "mess boy," washing and stacking the dishes, and cleaning out the galley and its pots and pans. It was all very informal and all very pleasant.

Each evening after supper there was a camp movie, for the Pole station had a stock of 500 films. You had to choose your film early and get it out from the corridor, for it took an hour and a half to unfreeze the film for showing. The same with the beer. Beer was unlimited, but it was no good suddenly saying you felt like a drink, then going to fetch it from the corridor beer store, for it would be as solid as a rock. Spirits were allowed for an hour or so each Saturday evening. They were on the house—the U.S. Navy—and consisted mainly of a remarkable brand of Bourbon whisky called Old Methusalem, best taken when mixed with tinned orange juice to disguise its rather peculiar flavor. We drank an awful lot of Old Methusalem that first night I was at the Pole, when the station held a small party in my honor—with a dinner of pork chops and three vegetables, followed by rice pudding. It was a wonderful feeling sitting there, not quite realizing I *was* there, surrounded by good companions in this wonderland of linking tunnels, planted and maintained by man for over a year in conditions so hostile that in five minutes outside the first morning my lips turned a real blue with cold, and in ten minutes taking photographs without gloves, the white of my fingers warned me of frostbite. Somewhat naturally, the attention of people at home was centered on the adventurous exploits of Fuchs and Hillary, but here too was an adventurous exploit that would probably in the end be of equally lasting value to mankind, and which was continuing, moving forward all the time.

Late on the first afternoon, Gus talked to McMurdo. The weather was excellent down on the Sound, and likely to remain so. But as it was so bad near South Ice, no contact could be made with Fuchs, and I was horrified that I might have to leave without speaking to him. Fortunately (from my point of view) when we walked outside the main hut, nature chose that moment to start an ice fog—something I would rather have seen from the other side of the window if the camp had had windows. It was like a light snowstorm, but as it was too cold to snow, it was formed of tiny ice crystals that bit into the exposed parts of our faces with diabolical fury. Even with this we could have taken off, but, as Shinn said, "If we had engine trouble on take-off, even minor, we couldn't turn back. Even two hundred yards from the Pole we would never find it again."

The next day, Saturday the fourteenth, it was still impossible to fly. But it was also impossible to contact Fuchs. For nearly an

hour the Pole radiomen tried to speak to him, but only a few un-
decipherable words came through, and finally we had to give it up.
Fuchs was still presumably battling up the ice wall, but a radio
blackout, the first of many I was to experience in Antarctica, cut
off all communications with him. Sometimes the blackout would
cut communications with the outside world for days at a time. We
could still get through to McMurdo, and I was on tenterhooks that
we might have to fly back before establishing radio contact with
Fuchs, the major reason for my flight to the Pole. I began to consider the possibility of requesting permission to stay on at the Pole,
even if the aircraft flew back, but it was not perhaps the wisest thing
to do. Communications from the Pole were very difficult, and I
wanted too to try and send a batch of photographs back to the office.
I would not have minded staying on a week or so, but from the
latest Fuchs position, it seemed likely that it would be some considerable time before he reached the Pole—and at that time there
was still no suggestion that Hillary would make his dash there.

Not that I minded the enforced stay at the Pole which the
bad weather was permitting me to enjoy. I had time to do all the
time-honored tricks which the Pole dwellers pointed out to me. I
walked round the world in three minutes, by circling the oil drums
and thus crossing every time zone on earth! I twiddled the fingers
of my watch haphazardly, knowing that wherever they rested, it
would be the right time, since every time zone converges on the
Pole. For the same reason I was able to set off in diametrically
opposite directions, safe in the knowledge that on each occasion I
was walking due north. This was all nonsense and fun, but then
everything was topsy-turvy. I found that all sorts of new values
manifested themselves, and all kinds of new irritations too. What
would one think was the most ubiquitous article at the Pole? Something I found stacked up in boxes ready for use everywhere. Paper
handkerchiefs. Without them life would have been utterly misera-
ble, for though there were no colds at the Pole, I only had to step
outside for two minutes and my nose started running. The sore
noses must have been terrible in the old days, for an ordinary

handkerchief wouldn't last five minutes against the running noses of polar living. A few moments of warmth, a few good blows on tissues, and it stopped.

Then I found that my lighter didn't work properly because of the altitude, and as I didn't at first like to diminish the supplies of the Pole's matches, life became a slightly mad effort to conserve my own matches. I couldn't buy matches because money didn't exist. There wasn't any at the Pole. There was a small shop, selling cigarettes, flints, and chocolate, but it did not even have anybody serving you. The stock was laid out in a corner of one hut, and when you wanted anything you were trusted to write down the details in a small book and sign for the articles. Presumably these notes eventually went to Washington and the totals were deducted from the men's pay, but money itself was never in evidence, so it was difficult for me, a casual stranger, to buy anything.

I found, too, I drank very little, largely because it was just too much trouble. When we had our hour of drinking on that Saturday night, we had to prepare the beer two hours beforehand, taking the tins of solidified beer and putting them into buckets of hot water by the stove. The Bourbon we drank either with orange juice or on snow, cutting a slice of snow from the block in the galley and putting it into a glass before pouring the whisky over it.

But perhaps the most irritating factor of all was the meticulousness required when I put things into pockets before venturing outside. Obviously I wanted to get out as much as possible. I found that so long as I did not walk too quickly at 10,000 feet, I could spend lots of time happily walking about, just taking in the fantastic desolate stretch of white, exactly the same whichever direction I took. But I soon found that when I dressed up to go outside, if I didn't put my things into the right pockets, life became almost unbearable. At the Pole, you fumble with mittened hands. Your goggles cloud up, the frozen fur from your hood gets into your mouth, your nose starts running and the stuff that runs freezes into an aggravating icicle—but all the time, because the hood comes right out in front of the head to protect it against the wind, you are like a horse in blinkers, seeing nothing to right or left. So you must work by touch—mittened touch. You can take your gloves off for a minute, but only a minute. You can take off your snow goggles and you will not go blind, but you won't see a thing for ten minutes when you go indoors. I never realized until I reached the Pole what a curse my reading glasses are. Normally, they are at hand in my breast pocket, but outside on the Polar plateau, I needed them each time I had to check the tiny figures on my exposure meter. This meant taking off my sun glasses and finding my reading glasses three layers down in my clothes. Then I would want to make a note of the photograph. That meant another pocket for pencil and note-book. If anything was in the wrong pocket, it meant nothing got done. All these movements had to be done with some semblance of speed because I was not specially trained for the swift transi-tion from Paris to the Pole, and though the temperature round about minus twenty may not seem to have been too cold, the thermometer could change with alarming speed, or a wind could alter the temperature effects on the body in a few minutes. Not long before my visit, the temperature was down to a hundred below zero and at that temperature it takes exactly ten seconds to freeze a man's face.

When I went down the snow mine to do my stint of cutting snow for water, the temperature was minus 61 degrees. Even though I had carefully smeared my lips with antichap lipstick (that valuable little tube no Pole dweller ever leaves behind) I found that after twenty minutes my outer mittens were as stiff as boards and my lips cracked like parchment. I wanted to photograph the snow mine with a fairly slow film instead of Tri-X, so for this I borrowed a bank of floodlights of the kind sold over the counter to amateur photographers. They were excellent, and I plugged the end of the flex into a convenient electric light socket, one of many at intervals on the way down the mine. I had enough trouble with my own camera fogging, but what never entered my head was the effect of the cold on the rubber flex of the lights, which lay on the snow. When I had taken my photographs and switched off the floods, the thickly insulated rubber flex just snapped like—I was going to say like a cotton thread, but it wasn't that, it had frozen stiff and broken like a thin piece of glass.

In between these pursuits, there was always plenty of time for good music, for the Pole had a library of classics I would dearly love to own myself. There were letters to be written and franked "South Pole," though one never knew when they would be dispatched. And there were innumerable cups of coffee with Gus and Vern and Mogy and the others, just talking to pass the time. Some of the men had been living at the Pole for more than a year. All of them were in their way celebrities with the American public, but they took their jobs very modestly even though the glamor of the Pole station was bringing them hundreds of fan letters from all over the world.

The most important concerned Dr. Fuchs and was received by Chet Segers, the cook, from an English lady—English mother of Vernon Houk. Segers was a wonderful cook—a matter of vital importance because breakfast, lunch, and dinner became the only clocks in a world that knew no dark and where time was on holiday. This letter read: "When Dr. Fuchs arrives at the South Pole you can be sure he will want a nice cup of tea. Please make it for him this way. Heat the pot inside and outside. Put in one teaspoonful of tea for each cup. When you have made the tea let it brew under a cozy for ten minutes. If you have no cozy, double up a pillow and tie it round the pot with the cord of a dressing gown."

When I last saw Chet Segers he was energetically undoing the tea from those monstrosities called tea bags and getting in some practice.

This lady was not the only Pole fan. When Vern Houk said casually that he saw no reason why he shouldn't try to start a garden at the Pole, scores of people airmailed him little bags of soil. Another woman sent the camp 1,100 bars of chocolate. A third —sadly misguided—sent the one thing of no value, a dollar bill, which was pinned to the camp notice board. But among these well-wishers, a new menace had sprung up. Since the cancelled stamps had a definite philatelic interest, hundreds of people were writing for letters bearing the Pole postmark. The record was held by a man from Texas who had already airmailed to the Pole packets containing a thousand envelopes, already stamped, to be sent back to him, suitably franked.

He was only one of the nuisances that impinged from the far-off outside world into the land of private white lives which I had so startlingly joined; a private world of timeless existence, intent on scientific research and the arduous business of staying alive, cut off, it was true, from the luxuries of life, but cut off also from the crises and curses of a world almost forgotten.

6. *In Touch with the Expedition*

On December 16, I made my first radio contact with the Trans-Antarctic Expedition, still battling heroically in wretched conditions before South Ice. For three days there had been a radio blackout, and Dr. Fuchs, never noted for the verbosity of his messages even during favorable conditions, had been out of touch with Hillary and with the expedition headquarters in London for some time.

When the omens for a radio conversation were good, I approached the task with considerable caution. Though Dr. Fuchs' contract to write for *The Times* did not preclude him from giving information to the press, the slow progress of his party had been shrouded in such secrecy that I felt instinctively any interference by other newspapers would not be well received. When Fuchs finally arrived at the Pole he could not have been more generous with the time he gave me, though he must have been dead beat after his long haul across the plateau.

But this was much later and after several reporters had managed to reach the Pole. When I first made my radio contact with Fuchs in mid-December I was the only one. Not even *The Times* had so far found it necessary to send a representative to Antarctica, for Fuchs himself was their correspondent. At this stage, therefore, one could readily understand a certain reticence on the part of Fuchs to see the latest details of his progress in a newspaper other than the one to which he was accredited.

Fortunately, one can always count on the Americans to help the press. I talked the matter over with Vernon Houk, then with Stan Greenwood, the operator on duty, and it was agreed that after the routine messages had been dealt with, Stan would tell the Fuchs operator there was an Englishman at the Pole who wanted to say hullo and wish the expedition good luck. I, on my part, determined to limit my questions to purely noncontroversial subjects. I did not need to question the position of the party; this I could determine from the routine messages which were passing through the Pole and which nobody could stop me from overhearing. I wanted, above all else, to gather some picture, however sketchy, of life on the ice, and, by talking later to Hillary or his rear headquarters, piece together the first accurate picture of the expedition's fortunes.

A curious incident preceded my radio talk. During the course of our conversation, Vernon Houk said casually, "It certainly looks as though Hillary will make the Pole long before Fuchs does."

"What makes you think he's coming to the Pole?" I asked.

"Wouldn't you—if you were in his place?"

It had naturally passed through my mind that Hillary—already at 700—might make a dash for the Pole, but I had not given the matter much serious thought. Later, though, there was a second incident: when the Pole station was speaking to Scott Base, I heard Stan Greenwood relaying a message from Houk, "Tell Hillary if he can make the Pole by Christmas, we are saving a bottle of champagne for him."

Soon after ten A.M. the Fuchs radio—called Shackleton Mobile— came through perfectly: "This is Shackleton Mobile calling South Pole—can you hear me, Shackleton Mobile calling South Pole."

To this Stan Greenwood, the tough 100 per cent American who was the Pole's chief radio operator, replied in a manner that for his race was truly startling. After identifying the station, he said in the most un-American way possible:

"We are receiving you loud and clear, old chap! How are you? Jolly good to hear you again, old man!"

Shackleton Mobile replied: "Morning, Stan. We are receiving you loud and clear, loud and clear. Over to you, old man, over."

It was all so casual, it might have been a couple of old friends talking on the phone about a game of golf.

I do not know how this short conversation strikes anybody reading it in cold print, but at that moment, sitting on an upturned biscuit tin with a notebook on my knees, and surrounded by the mysterious knobs and dials of modern radio, it sent a terrific thrill through me. To be sitting there in the radio shack, a pin point in a white desert, talking from the South Pole to these lonely men five hundred miles away on the ice could not leave me unmoved. Then I got a shock.

Stan said to the man on the other end of the schedule, "We've got an Englishman staying with us, old man, wants to say hullo to you, over."

Across the waves came a pleasant English voice, "That you, Noel! Glad to hear you made it! Yes, we heard on the BBC you'd reached the Pole. What's the weather like?"

"What's the weather like with you?" I asked. "Over."

"Well, the going's very rough and slow," came the reply. "We are just heading round the south end of Shackleton Mountain. We got through four crevasses yesterday all right, but we're certainly used to getting in and out of holes."

This was Ralph Lenton speaking to me, one of the expedition's radio operators. A month or so later Ralph and I toasted each other at the Pole. But Ralph was able to give me, in his free and easy fashion, all the details I required. One more Weasel, he told me, had fallen into a crevasse on the previous day, but had been recovered.

At the time I was speaking to them, Fuchs was inching forward on an inland ice shelf a thousand feet above sea level and slowly approaching the Shackleton range of mountains.

"After we get past this it should be fairly easy going to South Ice," said Ralph—but South Ice was still 500 miles from the Pole.

"Today," he added, "we are facing a big crevasse. We're having great difficulty getting round it, though it's a lovely day here."

As I sat there, talking backwards and forwards, I still could hardly imagine the Sno-Cats and Weasels plodding forward so many miles away while I chatted to them so casually about the weather.

So many varying reports about the expedition's speed had appeared in different publications that I asked Ralph outright what average he was making.

"On an average, about fourteen miles a day," he said. "One day we did sixty-five miles, but on other days we can only make one or two miles in a day; with our full load we can sometimes travel ten miles an hour, but more often it's seven, and sometimes it's down to three. Still, once we reach South Ice, we hope to step up our speed to at least twenty miles a day. With luck we should be at South Ice in less than a week."

The expedition did not reach South Ice quite so quickly as Ralph hoped. Ahead of them lay five more beasts of crevasses and many whiteouts which made it virtually impossible to proceed at more than walking pace, testing out the ground ahead. The crevasses covered more than twenty miles of closed broken country.

"When we get to South Ice," added Ralph, "we're going to have a rest of three days to work on our vehicles. We haven't had any really serious vehicle trouble so far, touch wood."

This was in itself a miracle, for, as Ralph told me, the vehicles were taking terrible punishment, and now for the first time I was able to piece together some of the fantastic work required to keep them rolling across the ice and snow, the work of two of the expedition's most tireless workers, thirty-three-year-old David Pratt and Roy Homard, of Sheerness, England, the engineers. Every 200 miles of the 2,000-mile crossing of Antarctica, these two men had to overhaul the vehicles in temperatures very rarely less than minus twenty—at which reading of the thermometer you can burn your hands when you touch metal. Each 200 miles they had to grease the 296 rollers of each cat, top up with oil all the differentials, gear boxes, and heavy working parts, then grease the 50 chassis and pontoon nipples, tighten the 130 track bars.

Over the radio a picture slowly developed. Their first trouble with the vehicles started when they were only 30 miles out of Shackleton Base at the very start of their trek, when the leading Sno-Cat, named Rock 'n Roll—which naturally took most of the punishment—suddenly dropped into a crevasse and fractured its chassis. The Sno-Cat was hauled out and Pratt and Homard jacked it up on planks—the planks being needed to stop the jacks from burying themselves in the snow under the 5,000 lb. weight of the vehicle. It took the two men a solid 24 hours of work, with only two breaks for tea, to repair the cat, which they did by disconnecting the two main springs and putting in a new plate.

Only four days before I spoke to them, said Ralph, the leading Sno-Cat, in which Fuchs and Stratton were travelling, found another wide crevasse which caused more bitter delay. Ralph gave me the bare outlines, but the details were filled in later by Fuchs, who said that 80 yards before reaching a flag marking the beginning of a crevasse zone, "we felt the well-known sinking feeling as the nose of the cat rose in front of us and the back sank deeper and deeper. For a moment we hung suspended by the sledge tow-bar, then tore off its four bolts and we dropped again till the back of the eight-feet-high body was level with the surface. On either side a yawning chasm had appeared and David Stratton and I had the problem of climbing out over the pontoons to firm snow."

This, said Ralph, was typical of the troubles that tortured the party before South Ice. Fuchs and Stratton could do nothing but wait until the other vehicles caught up with them. Then Fuchs learned that in fact he had broken through one crevasse after another, without realising it until the largest finally trapped them.

To their dismay, the engineers found serious fractures in the chassis. It took two days to repair or replace the broken parts.

Fuchs was finding that on the route to South Ice some of the terrain he had safely traversed on his proving trip in October was no longer so safe. The sun had so softened many crevasse bridges that they could no longer bear the weight of the Sno-Cats. It took Fuchs three days to probe a new route—and in doing so he almost smashed one of the four tracked pontoons of his Rock 'n Roll Sno-Cat. It took a day to make rough repairs, and Fuchs sent a message to Lewis asking him to fly out a new track pontoon.

"How is the air support under Lewis working out?" I asked Ralph. The answer was what I might have expected—it all depended on the weather.

In this case, bad weather grounded the planes for days—yet the engineers managed to keep the machines going in a climate of which Admiral Byrd wrote:

"Cold does queer things. At fifty degrees below zero a flashlight dies out in your hand. At minus fifty degrees kerosene will freeze, and the flame will dry up on the wick. At minus sixty degrees rubber turns brittle. . . . Below minus sixty degrees cold will find the last microscopic touch of oil in an instrument and stop it dead. If there is the slightest breeze, you can hear your breath freeze as it floats away, making a sound like that of Chinese firecrackers."

Yet Pratt and Homard kept the machines going—even once when a steering component broke. To mend it, they rigged up a pale green tent and instead of welding masks, each man wore three pairs of sun glasses. The punishment the vehicles were taking was staggering. And there would be much more to come, for though 1,500 miles of the journey was across the rough undulating ice-snow plateau, 300 miles of it was across *sastrugi*, the wind-hardened ridges of snow anything up to five feet high, while two hundred miles were crevassed areas.

"Mind you, it isn't all as bad as that," Ralph chuckled on the radio. "We've even had some days when we were stripped to the waist for sunbathing. We're all getting very sunburned. We look a bit grubby, but you can't really expect anything else, can you?"

No, it wasn't all like that, but it wasn't all sunbathing either, and each of the days was being fought out on a diet starting with five ounces of porridge and cocoa for breakfast, a cold lunch of meat paste or sardines and processed cheese with coffee or tea, and dinner of pemmican, curried, boiled, fried, or stewed, but always, always pemmican.

I was very tempted to ask if I could speak to Fuchs himself on the radio, but thought better of it. I would have been put in a very difficult position had he requested me to treat the talk as "off the record" and I should have had no choice but to comply. I thought it better to talk instead to the unsung heroes who were travelling with him.

Finally I asked Ralph, "When do you expect to reach the Pole?"

I heard one man chuckle, and another replied, "That's like looking into a crystal ball, but I hope once we have passed the mountains, we shall be able to make up our lost time."

The "lost time" was the critical phrase, for the team was a long way behind schedule. In fact, as Hillary was laying Depot 700, Fuchs should in theory have been approaching the same spot, yet he was even now weeks away from the Pole, in itself 1,200 ground miles from Scott Base. As I spoke to the expedition, Fuchs was 600 miles from the Pole, and seventy miles the far side of South Ice.

"Don't worry about us," said Ralph. "We're going to make it. Are you going to wait at the Pole for us?"

I told him I was not sure, but that I hoped, in any event, to return when Fuchs arrived.

When we had finished our conversation, Stan Greenwood took over to sign off; and again I heard Stan talking English. Finally, of all things, and perhaps without realising he was doing it, he said, "Well, cheerio until tomorrow, Ralph old boy. Toodle-oo and pip-pip and all that sort of thing!"

Quite obviously it would be a long, long time before Bunny
Fuchs reached the Pole, let alone Depot 700, for he still had the
wicked terrain before South Ice. Yet when I talked the same day
to Hillary's rear base, they told me he was roughly 500 miles
from the Pole, ahead on the plateau—that meant Depot 700—
with much faster and easier going than that which faced Fuchs.

"You see," declared Vernon Houk, "Hillary could get to the
Pole for Christmas if he wanted to."

But would he be allowed to? The relation between the two
explorers was quite clear. Fuchs was the leader of the expedition,
and Hillary was employed as leader of a support party, however
dangerous and invaluable his work was to be (and I doubt if Fuchs
could ever have reached Scott Base before the winter without Hillary's help). But wouldn't Hillary have to get permission from
Fuchs to "go it alone" to the Pole? I couldn't help wondering if
Fuchs would grant such a permission to a rival for hero's laurels, who
would by such a trip steal much of the leader's thunder. The feeling
at the Pole was certainly that Hillary would be crazy not to push
on to the Pole, but it was still a very tenuous feeling and perhaps
unwisely I did not take it very seriously. Not that it mattered.
There was still time for that hurdle when I came to it, if I ever did.

The weather improved, and flying was possible that night. I
seriously debated the advisability of staying on at the Pole, but I
couldn't see Fuchs arriving for at least three or four weeks, during
which time I might be much better employed at Scott Base or Mc-
Murdo, where communications were better. But the real factor
which decided me to leave was an uneasy feeling that if I made a
habit of talking to the Fuchs expedition, its members would be told
that, as a rival to *The Times*, I was *persona non grata* on their
particular air waves. It was a hunch, but it was a true one, for my
radio talk had an astonishing and swift repercussion, which could
have been aimed only at me. I naturally made the most of my talk
in my dispatches to London, where they were displayed with all the
vigor of a newspaper which has exclusive news of public interest.
In other words, in the language of Fleet Street, it was a ready-made

"scoop." Here was the first detailed news of the party's progress and how it was faring. It was naturally picked up from the *Mail* by radio and television stations, and the story itself syndicated to newspapers all over the world. Within a few hours the news had come back to Fuchs on the trail, presumably via the BBC. I had in my dispatches given accurate pinpointed positions of Dr. Fuchs' camps at various times, information of a later nature than any that appeared in *The Times*, for which the doctor was writing laconic dispatches when the mood took him.

This in itself scooped *The Times* as well as the rest of Fleet Street. I did not obtain this information from Fuchs himself, I acquired it merely by listening to the messages that Fuchs sent to Hillary via the Pole, and reading some of the back messages that had previously passed through the station. There was nothing wrong about it, as I knew full well before I ever set off for the Pole. The material was not classified as a military secret and, therefore, could not, by American Navy custom, be kept from the press. (At McMurdo, for instance, every single message in or out of the station was made available to the press and kept on a file for reference.)

But naturally the last thing that Fuchs ever expected was to have a British newspaper reporter at the Pole, listening in to his "conversations" with Hillary. I can understand his astonishment, which was no greater than mine at finding myself suddenly living at such an outlandish spot. But there it was. And reaction of the expedition leaders was swift. A message reached Vernon Houk, the Station Navy commander, requesting him to withhold all information about the expedition's position sent via the Pole station "from the press." Which meant of course me, as the sole representative at the Pole of our much-maligned profession.

Poor Vernon did not quite know what to do. He did not want to upset the expedition, partly because of his admiration for the work they were doing, and partly also because the Pole station was supplied from McMurdo, which was built on territory claimed by New Zealand, and anything in the nature of an international brush was, as I was the first to agree, something to be definitely avoided.

In the end Vernon did the only sensible thing. He sent the message forward to the Admiral for his comments, and Admiral Dufek replied as tartly as diplomacy would allow, with the following cable:

"It is not my policy to withhold nonclassified information from the press. Request you inform Dr. Fuchs and Sir Edmund Hillary not to send information to American stations which they do not wish to be made available to the press."

I must say that, though I could well understand Fuchs' desire to play fair with *The Times,* to which he was committed and which had supported him nobly, his request to the Americans was a trifle unreasonable in view of the use he was making of their station and men (a service gladly and unstintingly given by the Americans, I may add). Fuchs must also have realised that *The Times* alone was not paying for the Trans-Antarctic Expedition, but that public money from the British taxpayer's pocket had been generously accorded to finance the venture.

As far as the American aid was concerned, it must never be forgotten that the presence of the American Navy units and their aircraft made all the difference to the morale of the expedition. Though Fuchs naturally hoped to make this great achievement a purely family affair within the Commonwealth, he and his colleagues must have known all the time of the mighty strength that lay behind their frail human efforts, ready to be offered to save life and limb at the first request by the expedition. Though never begging for help, all along the trail, Fuchs and Hillary "used" the Americans in small ways—their radio, garage facilities at the Pole, a special flight to the Pole so that Hillary and Fuchs could meet, even medical supplies when one member of Fuchs' team was taken seriously ill.

The combination of this state of affairs was, of course, openly if politely discussed by the Americans. And when one takes into consideration as well that Fuchs was travelling on public funds, I think his request to the Americans about a solitary British newspaperman was a little ill-timed. I was, of course, bigoted—who would not be in my position?—but I always feel that when public money is being expended, the public has a right to know what is happening as the result of that expenditure—if somebody, in this case my newspaper, takes the trouble to find out. Fuchs had, it is true, made some arrangement so that Reuter's news agency could have emasculated versions of the dispatches sent by the temporary *Times* man at Scott Base, but, perhaps because of the delays in reaching the Pole, the expedition's progress was being kept just as secret as Dr. Fuchs wished until I came on the scene and by a very simple amount of reading and listening and putting two and two together, was able to give Britishers the first real details of what was happening.

However, on the other hand, one had to be fair. This was Fuchs' show, and (so long as he did not become a press dictator) he had a right to run it his own way. And nothing could have dimmed my admiration for the man. I decided, therefore—having, I must admit, one good exclusive story already in print all over the world—that it would be more courteous of me not to insist on "my rights." It was this, more than anything else, which made me decide to leave the Pole. I little knew that in a matter of days I was going to throw another monkey wrench into the intricate Antarctic works.

But firstly I had to return to McMurdo with Gus Shinn in the Old Charger, and when the whiteouts lifted and we prepared to leave (the first task being to heat the engines and oil with automatic heaters for two hours before we dared to turn the propellors) I said good-by to Vern and Mogy and the other boys at the Pole with genuine regret, and a considerable doubt whether I should ever see that strange little shed again. I had been immensely impressed with the Pole and the people who manned it in such alien conditions, and though it was obvious that Fuchs would in time reach its hospitable huts, getting up there myself was a much more doubtful matter. Weather during which men on the ice could advance might still preclude any flying, as for example in the past few days. I might easily be unable to greet Fuchs at the Pole—or Hillary if, as I was beginning to wonder, he decided to make a dash for it.

Vern and Mogy pressed me warmly to return. I had made many

friends there who, though short of the amenities of life, gave me farewell gifts that touched me deeply. Chet, the cook, found me a navy can opener, a fearsome instrument that now adorns my kitchen table and which opens cans automatically with an ease I had never considered possible. One of the meteorologists, Steve Fazekas, produced a lighter for me, engraved with a design to commemorate the Pole station and unobtainable anywhere else except at the Pole, very small supplies having been sent by an American firm.

But the trip back was to be much more than a "milk run"— it was a milk-bottle run in a whiteout that took all the resources of Gus to bring the Old Charger through. As we started, Gus said blithely, "Come on, Noel, let's see if we can make it!"

They were about the last cheerful words of the trip. The first thing that went on the flight back was the plane's heating system. At 12,000 feet above the plateau, it simply froze up. A short while later, after moving down towards the Beardmore Glacier, a white-out started, and in heavy, milky clouds with white sky meeting white snow, the radar froze up too.

We took off with the assistance of sixteen Jato bottles to help combat the thin atmosphere and extreme cold. Jato stands for Jet Assisted Take-Off. They are bottles of solid fuel, costing about $400 each, that are fastened round the outside of the belly of the aircraft rather like bombs and fired electrically. The pilot normally starts his run down the ice-strip, trying to make a little speed, and then when he thinks the moment ready to try to lift the aircraft off the ice, he presses the button that ignites the solid fuel. Each Jato bottle roars into activity, and gives 1,000 pounds of thrust for thirty seconds.

The force is terrific. Four bottles of Jato are roughly equivalent to one engine for the thirty seconds they burn. So when Gus Shinn pressed the button on sixteen Jatos as we gathered speed, it was as though the Old Charger suddenly had six engines instead of two. I had never experienced this before. I honestly thought the plane had blown up, the noise and vibration was so amazing; and just

Dr. Vivian Fuchs tells of the Expedition's plans during a press conference in London,
November 8, 1956.

Admiral Dufek, Commander U.S. Naval Forces in Antarctica.

Morton

U.S. Navy

Admiral Dufek's headquarters, officially called "Williams Air Operating Facility," but always known as McMurdo Sound.

What happens when the ice packs form quicker than you thought. Two U.S. Navy
ships trapped in the ice at McMurdo.

Home-made chapel at Mc-
Murdo camp, built by the
men themselves in spare
time.

Midnight sun at Scott Base.

Navy

The famous Dakota (DC$_3$) named "Que Sera Sera," but always known as the "Old Charger," in which Noel Barber made his first flight to the Pole.

Barber

Liv refuelling station, which must surely be the loneliest inhabited place in the world.

The U.S. Navy base at the South Pole.

The South Pole base as it looks from the ground.

*ton Beebe

Homemade Union Jack painted on a large white handkerchief which was hoisted with due ceremony at the South Pole beside the American flag and the flag of the United Nations.

Planet News Ltd.

American glaciologist at work in the South Pole snow mine. When Noel Barber took his turn, the temperature was minus 61 degrees.

Noel Ba

One of Sir Hubert Wilkins' assistants with some of the food left at Scott Camp in 1911.

Associated Newspapers

Scott's original hut.

Major Palle Mogensen examining a used Jato bottle with "Blizzard," the pet Husky.

Hillary's tractor team as it came into sight on January 4.

Sir Edmund Hillary on his arrival at the South Pole.

The 40-foot crevasse made when a tractor broke its parachute harness. Parts of tractor can be seen.

Huskies flopped in the snow on arrival at the Polar Base.

The entrance to the South Pole base.

Sir Edmund Hillary
and Dr. Vivian Fuchs
at South Pole Base on
January 20.

Morton Beebe

Lunch at the South Pole.

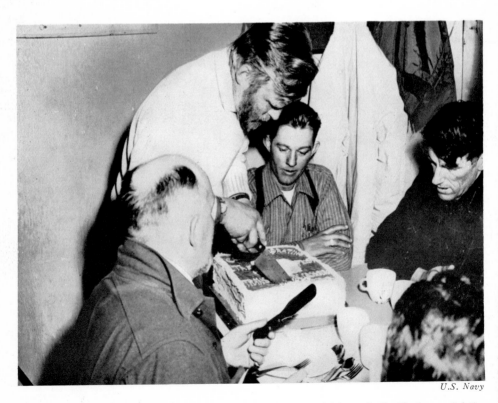

Dr. Fuchs cutting the special cake cooked in honor of his arrival. (*Left to right*) Palle Morgensen, Dr. Fuchs, Lt. Vernon Houk, and Sir Edmund Hillary.

The Neptune aircraft taking off. Ice crystals and Jato bottles make a trailing cloud of smoke and "ice-fog."

Noel Barber

Seals at Scott Base.

Noel Ba

The water creeping up near Scott Base.

beneath where I was sitting too! Crouching there, terrified out of my wits, I could feel unseen hands pulling the aircraft into the air, tearing her off the ice-strip which she hated leaving. Jato was one of the greatest flying aids in Antarctica. Indeed, without these precious bottles, so fierce that the flame from their individual exhausts used to scorch and burn the paint off the fuselage, we could never have flown to and from the Pole.

At first the weather was not too bad, but after an hour and a half, when the heater froze (it had only been partially working before that, and I rather fancy the prolonged stay at the Pole had more or less knocked it out of commission), the temperature dropped to minus twenty, and I began to feel my feet slowly going more and more numb. The navigator heated up a can of soup, but somehow it never reached all the way down to my feet. But Gus and his copilot were much worse off, for a small air inlet, bringing a current of fresh air past the heater into the aircraft in more normal circumstances, jammed open. The combined efforts of all of us could not close it. For the whole journey at 12,000 feet, a blast of icy air hit Gus around the legs and feet.

As for the radar, it just froze up, almost as we started to descend the Beardmore. We were in thick cloud. There was nothing to do but keep to the middle of this gigantic mystical gorge of jagged peaks, for without radar there was no way of telling just where those peaks were. Fortunately, we partly repaired the radar. The navigator came aft and pulled a long pole out of the litter of cargo. Then he squeezed forward with it, and gave the radar a hearty hit with the pole. Miraculously, it jumped into partial life, and started trembling. We were unable all the way home to get an entire circular sweep on the radar, but we did get a limited action, enough to keep us off the peaks on either side of us.

I do not suggest we were ever in really serious trouble. Gus was generally acknowledged to be one of the finest cold weather pilots in the United States Navy and he had a healthy respect for his own life, quite apart from the lives of others. I never saw Gus Shinn take a silly chance all the time I was in Antarctica. So we pressed on in thick whiteout and it really was like being submerged in a bottle of milk, and quite different from the cloud through which you often fly on commercial airlines. Sometimes we could see quite a long way through the "milk"—but the only thing we could never determine was where the cloud ended, where a white mountain started, or whether it was cloud or ground below us. It had a strange, translucent quality hard to describe. Ordinary cloud has its own characteristics. You can see it rushing past the wing tip of an aircraft in bad weather. It comes rolling over a plane. But this did not. I remember turning to the dentist and saying, "This must be the sort of cloud that angels loll on!"

As we approached Liv at the foot of the Beardmore, we tried to get the tiny station's homing aid, a primitive homing aid compared with those of modern aviation, but still a signal that would give us some indication of the whereabouts of this tiny dot. But we never were able to get her.

"We must be about over Liv," said Gus. "We've got enough gas to carry on, but I really think we'd better come down for an hour and warm our feet." Then he grinned and added, "That's what you'd call a British understatement."

The navigator managed to get a sunshot, which established our position fairly accurately. We were right overhead and started to come down quickly to sea level—the level of the Ross Ice Shelf. The Beardmore and all its dangers anyway were behind us.

"It's right below!" yelled Gus.

"How can you be sure in this cloud?" I yelled back.

"Hell!" cried Gus, "this isn't cloud. We're only seventy feet above the deck."

But Gus was wrong. We were zero feet off the ground. Almost as he spoke, we landed at nearly a hundred miles an hour on ice miles from the primitive runway. So thick was the whiteout—which meant a complete lack of any horizon—that it was impossible to tell accurately our height above ground. Ground and sky just met, that was all, but no man could say where. Our skis hit the ice with a terrific crack that almost shook the Old Charger to bits, but at least there is one thing about landing at Liv—once you are away from the Beardmore, the "runway" stretches hundreds of miles to McMurdo, for you can land anywhere on the shelf if you know how to do it.

With the incredible speed of Antarctic weather the whiteout suddenly lifted and a bright sun shone out across the white world. We had already started taxiing to Liv; we could see the two huts a few miles away: like blots of ink on a piece of white paper. It was also suddenly much warmer. Those 12,000 feet made a big difference. But as we stumbled out of the plane, I could hardly walk the first few steps. The crew followed to the tiny hut where the three men lived. It seemed an age since I had last been to Liv. They had coffee ready, thick chunks of bread and peanut butter, and we took off our boots and socks and, being careful not to get too close to the stove too quickly, slowly thawed out our feet. We spent a very happy and necessary hour at Liv.

"Well, that was a whiteout for you," grinned Gus. "Damn lucky you weren't in a helicopter. One got caught in a whiteout the other day and a crew member thought he was about to land and jumped out to fix the chocks. But when he stepped out of the plane on to what he thought was solid ground he made a slight mistake—and fell twenty feet."

After Liv we had a pleasant, easy flight back to McMurdo, and it was good to land on the ice-strip there, then walk up the road, half-mud, half-snow, to my own bunk again. I slept like a log that night until I awoke at six o'clock, and I remember the first thing that struck me as I looked at my watch was the sureness with which Vernon Houk had talked about Hillary going to make a dash to the Pole. I had better make the trek across the ice to Scott Base and see what John Claydon had to say about it.

7.   Back at McMurdo Camp

THERE was always a warm welcome for me at Scott Base, and I always enjoyed visiting it. Quite apart from the cozy atmosphere of such a small camp, I always felt McMurdo slightly out of place in Antarctica with so much mud and slush around. It was of course due to its exposed position, so that the small amount of annual snowfall was whipped away from the brown and black mountainsides by savage winds. But at Scott, so far and yet so near, the shelter of the surrounding hills kept it almost always white, and so packed with snow that, while I would go for a walk in ordinary GI boots up the mountains of McMurdo, the boys at Scott would be skiing down the opposite sides of the same hills.

The weather was much warmer, and the ice in the Sound was breaking up. No more Globemasters could fly in (lucky thing for me!) for the airstrip which they used was pockmarked with big holes, sometimes five feet deep, where the ice had melted. This was the Antarctic summer and, paradoxically, the warmth posed just as big a problem as the cold in winter. In the winter the machines were unable to fly from New Zealand, even though the airstrips were solid as dry land because of the cold. In summer the machines could fly, but the airstrips started to break up.

This applied only to the wheeled aircraft flying in from New Zealand, for at McMurdo we had two airstrips, which explains why I could fly where I liked in Antarctica, yet no other journalists could fly in to join me. One airstrip was for the heavy wheeled aircraft, the other for those fitted with skis. The Globemasters from New Zealand needed at least 5,000 feet of runway, but the DC3 and Neptunes (light bombers also used for the Polar run) were fitted with skis and could land on a much shorter strip. The runway for wheeled aircraft was out in the Sound itself, but the ski-strips were much closer to the shores of the island and, because skis were used, did not need to be so carefully preserved. A DC3 with skis would bounce over *sastrugi* that could smash up the undercarriage of a heavily loaded Globemaster.

The deterioration in the big runway was accentuated by the presence of smudge—anything black, oil droppings, black pipes, even a piece of dirty oiled rag. This had an alarming effect on the ice. When the hot sun beat down twenty-four hours a day on clean ice or snow, it caused no melting, as the surface automatically reflected the rays back into the air. But once the sun fastened on anything that was not white, it grasped the patch as it were with open arms, and started boring relentlessly down, causing serious melting. At McMurdo we had the crazy spectacle of able bodied seamen in gangs armed like charwomen with brushes and cloths cleaning up dirty patches on the runway. Even the black fuel pipe leading from McMurdo down across the ice to the runway had to have its position changed regularly, otherwise it began to sink in the ice. Sheets of tarpaulin had to be spread on the ice when big maintenance jobs were in progress to protect it from oil.

These problems did not affect Scott Base, for they only had the Beaver and the Otter which could land or take off in a few hundred feet, and they were within a quarter of a mile of enormous ice pressure ridges out in the Sound, where new ice and old ice, squeezed together, forced the ice into the air in jagged, fascinating ridges, rather like the way a plough forces up the earth. Seals played around here—anywhere close to a hole in the water—but the New Zealand aircraft were so light they were not worried by the proximity of ice holes.

All this made Scott Base a far more picturesque place, much more what one expected from Antarctica, not only because the camp was so small, but because it was also clean. The New Zealanders were able to dispose of their garbage in hidden places while McMurdo had huge piles of refuse, old tins, beer tins by the thousand, smashed-up cases, empty cartons. The garbage dump at McMurdo spread for nearly a hundred yards at the foot of the hill in full view of the camp, which was also littered with broken machines, tractors, sledges, left anywhere on the perimeter. None of these disfigurations spoiled Scott (nor the Pole, where Houk insisted that every morsel of garbage be buried). It was one of the advantages of living in small communities.

Unfortunately, John Claydon was not there. He had flown up in the Beaver to Depot 700 to see Ed Hillary. It was a great pity. The very fact that he had flown there presaged some news of possible import. I stayed for lunch—big, thick mutton chops, tinned apricots and lots of strong tea—and afterwards we played some Brahms on the long-playing phonograph. A radio message came from Claydon. He would not be back until midnight at the earliest. I read the daily cable that had come from Fuchs via the Pole. He was still stuck in a whiteout before South Ice. Hillary had caught up his dog teams, of course, and now was busy arranging the cache of food and fuel that would be ready for Fuchs when, or if, he ever reached 700.

These depots that Hillary had made (and the one that Fuchs had previously installed at South Ice) contained nothing but the most spartan supplies, and were primarily points carefully marked with flags and snow cairns at definitely identifiable points on the route, which could be seen by an approaching team from a long distance. They naturally also contained supplies of fuel and trail rations, and sometimes extra medical supplies. But little more, for

they were meant to be fuel depots and great time savers in navigation. If one could see the snow cairns of depots like 700 or 480 or
280 from twenty miles, it meant at least one day in which you could
get yourself right on course and not have to worry about navigation,
or crevassed areas, as the flag trails leading out from a depot were
always placed in lines that had been hitherto proved crevasse-free.
This in itself was a great time saver, as Fuchs was to find, for
crevassed areas in anything approaching whiteout conditions slowed
down the expedition to a walking pace—the pace of a man in front,
walking or skiing to test the ground ahead.

For some reason, and despite all the money spent on the expedition, Fuchs was not equipped with simple but fairly efficient
crevasse detectors that could have saved much time on the trail.
These had been developed by the Americans (who had also developed Fuchs' Sno-Cats) and consisted of a mechanical-electrical
device. As Dufek describes it in *Operation Deepfreeze:* "A plate
attached to a vehicle by a 12-foot pole rides ahead in the snow;
another plate is towed behind. The plates are connected to make an
electrical circuit. While the tractor travels over solid ice or snow,
the voltmeter has a constant reading. When the leading plate passes
over a snow bridge, the air in the crevasse changes the resistance of
the circuit, and the voltmeter fluctuates, with enough warning to
allow the driver to stop short of disaster."

It not only stopped a Sno-Cat short of disaster, but stopped
it short of time-consuming trouble. The time and trouble taken to
repair a damaged vehicle, to haul it out of even a small crevasse,
was much more of a problem to Fuchs than the danger of death.
Many crevasses were small, some many miles wide. Dufek summed
up crevasses more simply than any other writer in this way:

"A crevasse is a crack in thick ice or hardened snow, and can
either be open or covered by a thin bridge of blown snow—the
most treacherous of all. Some crevasses are only a few inches wide
at the top, and yet hundreds of feet wide below. Some are wide
enough to swallow up our largest equipment. Crevasses lie near
the edge of an ice shelf, in areas under tension where the ice is

forced around submerged rocks or islands, near the shore line or where ice streams merge and in foothills of mountains. New ones are constantly growing as the continental glaciers flow out toward the surrounding seas. In this world of ours the violence of nature seems to be accompanied by rare and great beauty. The beauty of a crevasse lies in its awesome stillness, the deep cold blue shadows. As I worked my way through several of these chasms, I was more chilled by a feeling of isolation than with the cold reflected from the brittle ice walls."

Even down by Scott Base, on the way back to McMurdo, there were small crevasses, for though both McMurdo and Scott Base were built on the shore of the same island, the pass through the mountain separating them descended, as a short cut, on to the frozen waters of the Sound itself, so that one passed by the airfield (naturally on the Sound, owing to the mountainous nature of the entire island) and then, without quite realizing where water ended and land started, since all was white, climbed back on to land again as the New Zealanders' base came into view.

As I walked back, disappointed at not seeing John Claydon for a heart-to-heart talk, I passed two crevasses, neither dangerous, but each utterly unknown in depth and underground size. One was a great gash in the ice, within fifty feet of the airfield, a crack six inches to a foot wide and at least a mile long. You could not miss it, and it was so narrow I did not even have to jump over it and—while I was there, anyway—there were no dark nights to worry about. A tractor tread would have ridden over it without noticing its existence. If a man had caught his foot in it, the hole was too narrow for him to fall in, and he might merely have turned his ankle. Like other crevasses I saw, it did not seem to spread in width, and caused no worries to the New Zealand pilots, blithely landing their aircraft within a few feet of it.

But a crevasse was also, technically, *any* hole in the ice, just as a *sastrugi* was any ridge of blown snow. Pilots landing at the Pole always talked of the care that had to be taken to land on the strip because of the crevasses—meaning not crevasses made by nature, but the holes caused by parachute dropping, including the one forty-five feet deep which a tractor had carved out when it fell from a Globemaster; it was carefully preserved, as a sightseeing tour, its rim marked with red flags.

There seemed nothing for me to do but attempt to pass the time as pleasantly as possible until news developed. I cabled the office that Claydon had gone to Depot 700. There was no point, I felt, in giving them the latest Fuchs position since it had been unchanged for some time, but I sent an informative message, not for publication, but for background, warning them that Hillary might at any moment make a dash for the Pole.

The time dragged heavily. The trouble with Antarctica was that every effort became just "too much bother." Even talking. Now that I am home again, people often ask me "What did you talk about?" The answer is "Very little." There were scientists who were extremely stimulating, but on the whole, when they came into my hut, or I visited them (whoever had a drink to offer) a serious conversation usually degenerated after a few minutes into a discussion of the quality of the last meal, or when Fuchs would arrive. Everybody's conversation was attuned to the lowest common denominator, possibly because of the lack of privacy. It was impossible to live in Antarctica and not be gregarious. So we would sit on the edge of a bed, drinking beer, and discussing politics or music or science, and in would bound some cheerful fellow looking for a drink, and that would be the end of that.

Because of the lack of room, there were no organised discussion groups, no places where one could relax. Vernon Houk at the Pole was hoping to cut down the number of movie shows at the Pole during the winter to three a week, and use the other nights for debates, but I very much doubted whether he was going to be able to do this, for, above everything else, the average Navy men looked forward to the nightly movie. Vernon did not like the men to show "big eye movies"—extra shows starting at 1:30 A.M., for those who could not sleep. Sometimes these were done if Vernon went to bed, but he rarely did retire before three in the morning.

But I discovered a most fantastic private theater at the Pole, rigged up so that three people could see a film if they had nothing else to do. It sounds incredible, but in the tiny projection box next to the Pole radio shack—a cubby hole four feet square containing the 16-millimeter projection machine—two men had rigged up a tiny screen with the aid of mirrors, roughly six inches square, on which they could, inside the projection box, show a film complete with sound (which could be turned down automatically). Time after time, I saw men crowded there—standing up three could squeeze in—absorbed in some ten-year-old Western.

No, we didn't talk much, and the members of both Hillary's and Fuchs' party told me later they faced the same problem. Life was too exhausting, even without heavy physical labor, to do anything that wasn't strictly necessary. Personally, I read from the small library; at McMurdo I read on an average a book a night, usually starting about nine P.M. and finishing in the early hours of the morning, then sleeping the morning away. One had to be a fixer to live comfortably in Antarctica, so I had managed to get a couple of old blankets from a departing sailor, and rigged these up as a curtain. From the naked bulb in the middle of the hut, I ran a length of flex to a bulb over the head of my bed, tied to a wooden lath on the side of the hut. I made myself a rough lampshade (which had to be replaced regularly when it burned where the bulb touched it) and tucked myself in. I had my own glass, and under the bed a supply of orange juice; life wasn't so bad. It was just dull, for people like myself who did not have work to do all the time.

"Dull!" exclaimed the dentist who had flown up to the Pole with me. "Hell! you should be in my job!" But that would have been carrying things to the other extreme, for the dentist was the most overworked man in McMurdo. He not only dealt with the camp personnel, which was constantly changing, but had to fly when necessary to any camp to deal with urgent cases of toothache —providing always it was possible to fly. A serious dental problem during the Antarctic winter could have really dire results. At the Pole, during the seven months when the station was cut off and it was quite impossible for any aircraft to fly in, one man broke his false teeth. For weeks he tried to carry on. No dentist could be flown in, and because it was virtually impossible for the cook to make a special diet for him, he lost forty pounds in weight. He just could not masticate all food provided, and the doctor at the Pole finally managed to hold a voice conference on the radio with the dentist at McMurdo, who gave the Pole leader a running lesson in how to mend the man's plate. In the end it was stuck together with aeroplane glue, and had to last like that until dawn broke several months later.

The dental fillings had to be most carefully done, for the bitter cold had one odd result on dentistry—which I found out to my own cost. If you were working outside and talked too much, the cold contracted the filling which then dropped out. I lost one that way, fortunately not one that caused any pain. At McMurdo the dentist was the busiest man in the camp, for he was the only one. I never dared to ask him what would happen if he ever got toothache himself.

The lonely doctors like Allan Rogers on the trail with Fuchs, or Vernon Houk at the Pole, faced the same problem—what to do if they fell ill? Vernon received one of the most disheartening anonymous letters any doctor cut off from the world could possibly receive, containing detailed instructions, obviously from another doctor, on how to take out his own appendix.

There were always dangers of serious accidents—industrial accidents much more than occupational diseases. One man broke both his elbows in a tractor accident. Others were badly burned, some in plane crashes. The doctors on the trail always managed to patch them up.

We did not have much illness. During all my time in Antarctica, only one serious illness struck McMurdo—a case of infectious hepatitis, dealt with so swiftly it never spread. It is not a dangerous disease, but it attacks the liver, so the doctor told me, gradually weakening the patient, who has to rest for many weeks, and lay off alcohol. A New Zealander's wife caught it and was taken to hospital in Christchurch. Unknowingly, he contracted it from her. It was diagnosed at McMurdo, and within an hour every single cup and plate had been locked away, and the man isolated until he could be evacuated. For six weeks we ate from cardboard plates and cups. Otherwise, because of the lack of germs, we were all as fit as fiddles. Indeed the only time men in Antarctica caught a cold was when they received a packet from home, which brought germs along.

On the third day after my return I broke the monotony with a fascinating excursion into the Antarctica of yesterday. The weather was beautiful, the temperature plus five, no wind, a vivid, aching sun. A helicopter was making a trip to Cape Evans, twenty-five miles or so along the Ross Sea, facing the open sea from the other side of Ross Island. Would I care to go along? I most certainly would. We spun out in the chopper, always so much more exciting than flying in an ordinary aircraft, and half an hour later landed on a patch of black earth, sending up swirls of dust, within ten yards of the black water of the Ross Sea. Near by were three small nylon bivouac tents, each big enough for one man. Fifty yards away was an old wooden shack.

This was the base established by Scott in 1910, and living there temporarily was one of the grand old men of Antarctica, Sir Hubert Wilkins, now sixty-nine, but as tough as leather, who probably knew more about the Antarctic than any man alive. He had flown out to Cape Evans to spend some time there with two companions living in tents and eating nothing but dehydrated survival rations to test their effects on men. I looked forward to an incredibly bad meal, but I could not have been more mistaken.

The helicopter whirred into action, blanketing us in black dust —dust in the Antarctica, it really was too ridiculous—with the promise of returning to pick me up later that day.

Wilkins, sporting a trim goatee beard and with a nose which the cold had turned as red and shiny as a small apple, was a most engaging character. His tests with dehydrated food, he explained, were over. He was now camping at Cape Evans for a few days longer while his companions collected geological specimens and he took a holiday. Next to his small camp stood the solid wooden shack that Scott had planted there forty-seven years ago, still in excellent condition, though filled with packed snow so that one could not enter. The bones of some of his Manchurian ponies lay around.

"But I'll give you a meal you'll never forget," said Wilkins, and he most certainly did, for I ate the strangest meal of my life, a meal cooked and tinned at least fifty years ago, but which, due to the natural refrigeration of the Antarctic, was just as good as new. When Wilkins arrived at Cape Evans he found an enormous cache of food in tins left by Scott in case of emergencies. How little the Antarctic really changes, for at this very time the descendant of Scott and Shackleton, Sir Edmund Hillary was doing just the same thing, laying in food stocks at depots along the trail.

At Cape Evans, there seemed to be everything. We opened a tin of cooked mutton, heating it on a modern cooking tablet from the American survival ration bag, and followed this with some excellent Stilton and biscuits. Then some more biscuits and marmalade—the very same brand of Oxford marmalade I eat at home each morning, and in just as good condition.

The meal was excellent and there were hundreds of tins of it. The cheese was rather high, and tended to crumble when we opened the tin, but it was quite edible. The biscuits still retained much of their original crispness. There were scores of tins of English vegetables, some wonderful greengage jam (I tested that too), boxes of Quaker Oats, Cerebos salt, and Coleman's mustard in huge tins and all in well-nigh perfect condition. The only thing that had gone off was some corned beef.

The store of food was not buried. Scott had left it in a small hollow halfway up the hillside and surrounded by snow. This had kept it in almost perfect condition, and the natural dehydration of the Antarctic air had stopped it from going bad. We found bars of chocolate, even some old showcards for Fry's, and when I was rummaging around, I opened a carton of ordinary boxes of matches which I struck into a flame without any trouble. I would have sorely liked to take back a selection of souvenirs—there were so many, nobody would have missed any—but the thought of overweight from New Zealand to London prevented me. I did take some boxes of matches though, remembering how short of matches I had been at the Pole when my lighter refused to work. They would be very useful if I returned. (They were also very useful on my return to England when I lost my lighter.)

It was a wonderful, happy afternoon, hand in hand with the past. I would have dearly liked to remain at Cape Evans ("Stay by all means," offered Wilkins, "I'm sure we have a spare tent!") but one of the chores of being a reporter is that you can't always do what you want. You can be the best newspaperman in the world and it will avail you nothing if you do not keep open your lines of communication and make your daily checks on news that might develop at any moment. So the helicopter flew me back into the present and more hamburgers for supper at McMurdo, and to pass the evening I went, as usual, to the camp cinema for my nightly hour or so of stale romance (each film being up to ten years old).

What else was there to do? The days idled by in McMurdo. The tunes on the camp radio were too well known. The library books had been well thumbed. The few walks across the snow or black volcanic rubble had lost their charm if every they had any. Even the fantastic view of the white-clad mountains across the Sound were by now to me as dull as a Christmas card of the Alps that had arrived in June. And as every day dragged along on feet of lead, the movies at least got rid of those last hours before one turned into a sleeping bag to try and cheat monotony of eight hours.

There were problems, I admit, the main one being that the seating was so bad (either at the mess tables if one came half an hour early, or else stretched on the floor) that with all the craning in the world, the shadows of those in front tended to turn even the pride of Technicolour into a film of large black shadows. After seeing the other half of the screen, there were many who considered that the men in front casting their shadows before them were rendering a public service, but on the whole I enjoyed McMurdo Movie House, stretched out on the floor, changing elbows when I got tired, for in between the bad films wonderful fingers stretched out and beguilingly beckoned me to an almost forgotten past. There was something eerie—and indefinably sad—about yesterday's heroes tugging at today's heartstrings. Fred Astaire—not looking a day over fifty—dancing with a wraith of forgotten beauty whose name it appeared was Ginger Rogers, to tunes that tore away the cold shroud of the present and thawed me with happy, nostalgic memories. Old friends were back, old friends you would never meet except at McMurdo Movie House. The one and only Bogart, behaving like a human being and a gangster before he got mixed up with the Caine Mutiny. And Garbo—I even saw her again one evening, back to the days when she was an actress and not a legend. Yes, I liked it when supper was over, when the cook in the chowhouse drew the flimsy screen across the self-service counter, and the lights were dimmed and the old projector cranked away and took me to friends I never thought I would see again.

That night, after I returned from Cape Evans, we showed, I remember, *Magnificent Obsession*. It was a date I was to remember, December 21. Was it only four days since I had left the Pole? It seemed like four years. We trailed out of the cinema into the vivid white night and I went to see where I could scrounge a drink.

In my hut was John Claydon, wrapped up in his parka, goggles pushed up over his forehead. It was always wise to dress up for the walk between Scott and McMurdo—you never knew what would happen to the weather. He sat down on the edge of my bunk and we found a couple of cans of beer that were not frozen, punched holes in their lids, and drank from the cans as usual.

"Well," I began, "what's the news about Hillary? Is he going or isn't he?"

John Claydon hesitated.

"You know it's difficult for me, I can't say officially anything about the movements of the expedition, though I must say I think all this secrecy is rather silly."

"Well, what do you think—you yourself?"

"Hillary has gone forward from 700——"

"You mean he has actually left—gone to the Pole? Why, that's terrific!"

Claydon grinned and took another drink of beer.

"I didn't say that at all. He might be probing crevassed areas near 700. He might be doing one of a dozen different things."

"What do you think?" I insisted.

"What would *you* think, with all that extra fuel flowing up to Depot 700—far more than Bunny asked Hillary to leave there? What would you think Hillary would do in a position like his, with at least a month to wait for Fuchs to arrive?"

I knew John well by now. I knew he was trying to tell me enough facts for me to make my own decision. But I did not like to "go out on a limb" for such a big story, a story that would hit the world's headlines, unless I were absolutely sure.

"I know I can't quote you, John," I said, "on a definite statement that Hillary is off to the Pole, but can I quote you on something? Is there one sentence, which wouldn't be official, that we could print?"

He thought it over and then, because he was essentially a matter-of-fact man, said, "Yes, there is. You can say this. You can say that it is my personal—but you must insist on the word 'personal'—it is my personal opinion that Ed will finish up at the Pole."

That was enough. It was more than enough. The race to the Pole between the two giants, at opposite ends of Antarctica, was on. That night I filed what I think was the best story I ever sent from Antarctica, starting out, "Sir Edmund Hillary has set off for the South Pole. Last night with three tractors and four men, he left Depot 700," then adding the covering note, "Squadron Leader

John Claydon, of Hillary's rear headquarters at Scott Base, told me, 'My personal opinion is that Ed will finish up at the Pole.' "

It was a terrific story and, being a Saturday, I had lots of time to assemble my facts, trace the route, and assess the problems involved. Hillary was on his way! And so the original plan of Fuchs to cross Antarctica with Hillary in a purely supporting role on the way home was suddenly turned into a dramatic "race" by two British teams to be the first men to reach the Pole by land since Scott. For, as I worked out the positions on the map, why couldn't Fuchs make it as well?

On this day, only a few days before Christmas, how did the two teams stand?

Fuchs was, according to the latest messages, still held up by whiteouts the other side of South Ice. It would take him two days to reach South Ice, which was 500 miles from the Pole. He was, it is true, hemmed in by filthy weather and had been snowbound for several days. But if the weather lifted, and it could lift in an hour if it chose to, Fuchs could set off at great speed on a race across the Polar plateau, only two days behind Hillary.

Hillary, it appeared, was thirty miles south of Depot 700, so he was already about 470 miles from the Pole. He had the great advantage of travelling lighter than Fuchs, of doing none of the scientific work which took up so much of Fuchs' time. If Fuchs wanted to get to the Pole first, he would probably have to cut down heavily on his scientific program, something which I doubted very much that he would even remotely consider. It looked as though Hillary would certainly win this "race," if it were ever to be considered a race, but one never knew. Once on the plateau, Fuchs could make 40 miles a day as easily as Hillary if he had good luck. And there were all sorts of imponderables. Who could tell whom fate would favor? Hillary could smash one machine and Fuchs could win, or else the opposite could happen. Fuchs could have a man injured on the trail, and Hillary would romp home. It was like an extraordinary obstacle race in pitiless conditions, with all sorts of extra hazards thrown in, as though the battle against ice and snow and whiteouts were not enough.

Late into the Antarctic night I worked at the rough desk made from old planks where I had installed my typewriter and papers. There were all sorts of other questions to be answered if a complete picture were to emerge.

Hillary was on the way—that was the first thing. How was he equipped? He had his three Fergusons, supplies for one month, plus a large stock of survival rations. He and his radio operator were sharing the caboose which Hillary himself had designed, while the others slept in tents. Hillary's caboose was drawn on a sled and had two bunks, the radio equipment and a certain amount of heat denied to the other members of the team. It was very narrow (as I saw for myself later), but it had some semblance of comfort. Here Hillary and his operator, Peter Mulgrew, lived, mainly on bacon and scrambled powdered eggs (as Hillary couldn't stand pemmican). Murray Ellis, an engineer, and Derek Wright, a cameraman, shared a small polar tent. They too did their own separate cooking by primus stove in the square shaped tent, its corners held down by snow. The fifth member of the team, Jim Bates, was, until Depot 700, sharing a tent with another expedition member who then returned to Scott Base, so Bates had a tent to himself.

It may seem odd that these men, bound so closely by the appalling conditions in which they lived, should each be living separate lives, cooking in their own tents, and that one of them should even be alone, deprived of all companionship, but the reason was of course that once Hillary reached Depot 700, at an altitude of more than 8,000 feet, it became so bitterly cold that all cooking had to be done in the tents or the caboose.

There were many questions to be answered. Did Fuchs know of this dash by Hillary? He must, surely. Did he approve of it? What cables had been exchanged between Hillary and Fuchs? And, above all else, whether or not Fuchs gave his permission, should Hillary have made the attempt? Was it the right thing for a second in command to go ahead like this?

Already there had been rumors. Mr. Charles Bowden, chairman of the Ross Sea Committee, which directed the New Zealand party, said Sir Edmund might go to the Pole. Asked to comment on this, Mr. Walter Nash, the New Zealand Premier, said, "If Sir Edmund wants to go and if he feels it is safe for him to do so, then I see no reason why he should not go. I think it would be a good thing for him to add the South Pole to Everest. But I don't want him to do anything which might mean his not coming back to New Zealand."

Bowden said Sir Edmund and his party, now that they had reached the rendezvous point, were to all intents and purposes free agents. Their present task was to stock the base and explore the hinterland.

"Sir Edmund might move into the interior of the Pole if circumstances of the, up-to-now, slow-moving British side of the expedition demanded it. A great deal will depend on the progress by the British in the next day or two."

But that did not answer any of the questions posed above. They were all going to be answered, however, by a strange (and most unfortunate) release of a private message from Hillary.

Already, though, there were several unrelated conversations, which I began to remember, that lead me to believe Hillary was always hoping to make the Pole, and bring off a brilliant double, that this was a premeditated dash, not something done on the spur of the moment. When I was in Christchurch, several New Zealand journalists who had been in Antarctica at Scott Base previously and very close to Hillary, had told me without any shadow of doubt that Hillary was going to "have a go" for the Pole. Leslie Hobbs had warned me to be ready for this very moment. Nobody ever suggested that if Fuchs had been on time at 700, Hillary would not have been there to receive him, Pole or no Pole, but Fuchs had been behind schedule all the way along the expedition, and Hillary had known for months that he would have spare time to fill in while waiting. John Claydon's attitude was, basically, "Well, why not? He's done his job. What else could he do?"

At this stage I did not know all the details of Hillary's dash to the Pole. I was to find out more when I met him there. And in view of the meager information I had, it was also too early to answer the question, "Should he have done it?" The opinions on the moral right of Hillary to make the Pole dash were always strictly divided in Antarctica. There were as many who frowned on his attempt as there were who applauded it. Many felt at least he could have waited (but where? one asked) until Fuchs was nearer the Pole, so that the two could perhaps have reached the Pole from opposite ends of Antarctica together. But an equally large proportion took the attitude that Fuchs anyway was engaged on a scientific expedition in which the South Pole was a minor point to be passed on a much more important journey, and if one of his assistants had a few weeks on his hands, why not let him do it?

There were other questions—but of these I knew nothing as yet. It was enough that Hillary was on the way.

Now, I had to get up to the Pole again—and in double quick time. I had always hoped to return, for, though no British reporters were able to fly into Antarctica, I had there as companions three Americans from the Associated Press, United Press, and *New York Times*. They had understandably been more concerned with American activities in Antarctica than with the Trans-Antarctic Expedition; and though I had gone to the Pole alone, leaving them at McMurdo, this was because they—from the American point of view—preferred to fly up and write a story about Christmas at the Pole, whereas I had gone to be able to talk to Fuchs.

I had, however, while saying nothing, always hoped to join them if the chance came again. And it did. A plane was scheduled to fly up with more mail—and a Christmas tree—and room for the four of us was found on it.

The mail arrived on December 22, by the only other Globemaster to fly in from New Zealand before the weather got colder. Though my Pole story had been in print for nearly a week, fortunately (from my point of view) no other English reporter had managed to get himself accredited to the Americans and fly out in this brief time. Two New Zealanders, one of whom was working part-time for *The Daily Telegraph*, were on their way by icebreaker and just missed their "connection," so once again, as far as the British press was concerned, I was on my own for Christmas, and for Hillary's arrival.

8. *At the South Pole*

I REACHED the South Pole for the second time on December 23, to find the station alive with the spirit of Christmas, and alert with expectancy now that Hillary was definitely on his way. I flew up this time in a Neptune, a twin-engined light bomber, with two auxiliary jet engines that could be switched on at will to give an extra boost for rapid climbing. It was a very uncomfortable aircraft, and I had to sit on the floor for five hours. The Neptune, piloted by Jack Coley, the commander of VX6, the U.S. Navy's experimental air squadron, dumped us on the snow at the Pole and flew back to McMurdo almost immediately. I would stay this time at least a couple of weeks until the next plane came in the New Year, bringing mail already on its way by icebreaker.

Christmas at the Pole was a festive affair among old friends. Vernon Houk and Mogy and some of the boys even provided presents for me, which were handed out by "Zeke," the meteorologist, who played the part of Santa Claus. I had saved a bottle of Scotch for the occasion, and we even had a Christmas tree which I brought up on the plane with me, but which was partly ruined when Blizzard, the only huskie at the Pole, ate half of it.

(An amusing version of the ruined Christmas tree appeared in the *Daily Mail*. I cabled that it was partly eaten by "a huskie called Blizzard." Somehow the word "called" got lost in transmission, and so the story came out in London that the tree was ruined, partly by a huskie and partly by a blizzard!)

But the *pièce de résistance* at Christmas was an enormous candle made by the same Zeke, who spent hours patiently mixing large quantities of paraffin with an electric egg beater until it had the consistency of whipped cream, so that he could then "sculpt" a candle, later to be decorated with tiny pieces of colored tinsel paper. The living-room was decorated with Christmas-tree lights, and knee-deep in chocolates and fruit cakes, many of them parcels from anonymous donors. I was very touched when several of the Pole team—and not the officers only—crossed their names off the parcels sent to them and substituted mine, for it was obviously impossible for me to receive parcels in time.

I tried desperately hard to telephone on the "ham" amateur radio to England or France, where my wife was spending a lonely Christmas, but to no avail. I spoke to an amateur radio operator in Milan who promised to telephone Paris, and then, out of the blue, my old colleague from Budapest days, Jeffrey Blyth, managed to get through to me from New York. We talked for a quarter of an hour, then he, finding it difficult to reach the small country village where we had established our home in France, telephoned Tony Brown of the *Daily Mail* in London (later to relieve me in Antarctica) who in turn telephoned my wife. She had my Christmas messages within twenty minutes of my speaking to Jeffrey from the Pole.

The BBC from London made frantic efforts to reach me, so that my voice could be included in their round-the-world Christmas day broadcast. It was an excellent idea, but though the Americans were talking backwards and forwards from the Pole to their families, regulations in Britain made such action quite impossible. There was no telephone as such at the Pole. These conversations, like mine with Jeff Blyth, were organised by a 17-year-old student, Jules

Madey, of Fulton, New Jersey, who for a year had been operating an unofficial "telephone exchange" for the South Pole scientists and their families in the United States. A simple gadget he had fitted to his radio receiver enabled him to link his one kilowatt set with the local telephone system. That meant that once he had located me on the "ham" radio at the Pole, all he had to do was telephone Jeff at his New York apartment, reversing the charge, and plug him in to me. This could only be done with the blessing of the American authorities. No such blessing was available in Britain, unfortunately.

The long night wore on with music on a portable piano, an ingenious contraption that had been parachuted down and folded up like a suitcase, light enough to be carried a short distance by one man. Since my last visit, the station had unpacked another plastic hut which had been turned into a recreation room, complete with a small billiard table, also dropped by parachute. Really, we were becoming quite civilized! But all the same, as I wrote in my diary that night, "Through all the fun and crackers, I think almost everybody was thinking of home, and nothing but home. The boys really did their best. Zeke, a meteorologist, who is the largest man in the camp, made a fine Santa Claus, and handed out presents to everybody, including myself. Vernon, the Navy commander, bought us a case of champagne, and somebody had sent one of the boys one single wonderful box of Havana cigars, which he immediately handed round for everybody. We had a truly fabulous dinner, including caviar, roast turkey, a whole baked ham, corn meal, candied sweet potatoes, asparagus, all sorts of sauces, and finishing with plum pudding, mincemeat tart, and pumpkin pie. We even had menus, and I was very touched by the fact that the boys had typed out a special one for me."

This special menu was the result of a mistaken notion that I had the largest appetite ever seen at the Pole, an idea which was disproved (or was it?) by the fact that I lost ten pounds there. But it was their idea of a compliment to me, for I got on very well indeed with all the boys. The menu was headed

South Pole Station
(Also known as Barber's Pole)

and contained such extraneous remarks as Caviar (Barber had some); Turkey (Barber stuffed himself); buttered potatoes (Barber ate); fresh asparagus (Noel Barber still going strong); pumpkin pie (Barber began to get down to serious eating); and at the bottom the libellous phrase "Noel Barber complained to cook not enough chow."

The only thing that went wrong with the evening was that the cinema show after dinner was delayed for an hour, while the film had to be unfrozen.

As we enjoyed our simple festivities so far from home, Hillary was bounding along. By December 26 he had only 325 miles to go, while at the other end of Antarctica, Fuchs had passed South Ice, he was over the hump, and about 450 miles from the Pole.

Hillary's advance in the early days of the dash was phenomenal and, in two days of marching, he made more than a hundred miles. There was no holding back in his nightly drive forward, with a record of fifty-seven miles covered on Christmas night. (Hillary was driving by night because the sun was then directly ahead of him, making it easier for him to take sun reckonings for navigation. It did not matter, naturally, which hours of the twenty-four he chose to sleep.)

On December 26 he spoke to Scott Base but we at the Pole were unable to pick him up. He radioed: "We are heading hell-bent for the South Pole, God willing and crevasses permitting."

The weather was good, he said, and the party were all fit, adding:

"The march of two nights ago was the first time we had not seen or fallen into crevasses, and the magnificent leap forward of the past few days has made it possible for an earlier attempt to reach the Pole than was originally planned. Now that the days of uncertainty and doubt are over, a new enthusiasm has seized the expedition's members who have been working long and hard for such a moment."

This quaint phrase at the end indicated once again that, always at the back of his mind, Hillary had determined to reach the Pole.

But, whatever the outcome, the achievement was building up into an exciting drama. For years people will argue whether Hillary should have gone to the Pole or not, but right or wrong, with what magnificence he was making the trip. His Ferguson farm tractors, small twenty-six horsepower machines which nobody ever before considered suitable for Polar work, behaved magnificently. Because they were sitting mostly with the weight on the back, they were proving unexpectedly safe for crossing crevasses.

As Hillary lumbered on, communication with Fuchs was still difficult, but at least he was now well beyond South Ice. One message received from him said he hoped to see us "soon," but about this time, Fuchs, because of the shrinking distance between the two parties, managed to contact Hillary directly on the radio, and so we did not have the same communications with him at the Pole as before.

But already there were signs of trouble ahead for Hillary. On the Pole radio we listened in to the New Zealand news. According to one report, popular pressure had already mounted in New Zealand to free Hillary from his "obligation" (if there ever were one) to stay at 700 for Fuchs, and a report on the radio said that Bowden, of the Ross Sea Committee, had radioed Hillary to get in touch with Fuchs to talk it over. But then, according to a news report I heard on December 26, Hillary had "defied" the orders of his expedition's New Zealand Committee, and the same Mr. Bowden was reported as saying that he had received no official advice from Hillary about his decision to push on to the Pole. When asked if the decision was taken with the committee's permission, Mr. Bowden answered, "I am not going to answer that," and when questioned about the possibility of halting Hillary even now (a slightly ridiculous suggestion and very hard to put into effect)

Bowden answered, "Well, he is going apparently. Sir Edmund is apparently satisfied that his resources are adequate, and presumably the revised arrangements are the result of discussions between him and Dr. Fuchs."

Presumably so. In London, Rear-Admiral Parry, secretary of the expedition's headquarters, insisted, "Dr. Fuchs will certainly not try to race ahead if he has time in hand. He has a complicated scientific program to carry out, and he will want to give all the time he can to that."

At the Pole, wagers were being taken that Hillary would reach the bottom of the earth by New Year's Day, but these hopes gradually faded as Hillary started to run into soft snow and his speed slowed up considerably. By the last day of 1957, Hillary was still 150 miles from the Pole. We picked up his exact position—87 degrees, 40 minutes South, longitude 141 degrees East. The steady rise in altitude to nearly 11,000 feet was resulting in a considerable reduction in the power of his three tractors and Hillary was seriously considering abandoning some of his fuel and stores.

As Hillary moved forward, another drama was being enacted, one which, because of the more dramatic dash by Hillary, never really received the public praise which was its due. This was the flight from South Ice to Scott Base by Squadron Leader John Lewis, in a single-engined Otter aircraft, a remarkable achievement.

The Otter, with Lewis as its top-hatted pilot, was Fuchs' support plane at South Ice, and once Fuchs was past South Ice, and safely on the way to the Pole, there was no point in leaving this light plane behind. It was agreed, therefore, that Lewis should try to make Scott Base. This was a great flight, for the Otter was not heavily enough powered to land at the Pole altitude and ever hope to take off again. John Lewis had to go the whole way alone in steadily worsening weather as the winter approached.

On December 30, as Hillary reported his latest position, with the added information, "The weather is still fine but the cloud is increasing and temperatures are much colder," John Lewis called us up. With Fuchs now between South Ice and the Pole, he felt he could fly on. His radio could not possibly call Scott Base, so we laid on a meteorological report for him that covered him from the Pole to Scott. The weather at the Pole was fair, not perfect as I saw it so often, but good enough for flying. Lewis would not land, but he would fly overhead and we would talk to him on the radio.

This historic flight—doomed to failure on the first attempt—started at half past ten in the morning (coming from the other side of Antarctica, Lewis was flying in daytime, and so would have the same benefits from the sun as Hillary had by moving at night). At first all went well. The tiny aircraft made excellent progress on his flight of 1,280 air miles from South Ice to Scott, while two Otter aircraft attached to McMurdo planned to go out and meet him on the Ross Ice Shelf and escort him to base. But by one o'clock, he was in serious trouble. By two P.M., when he should have passed the Pole, the aircraft was building up rime ice in thick cloud which was unbroken to 15,000 feet. The machine began to lose height. Pitifully, everywhere else along his track the weather was fine, with only scattered cloud and no turbulence or ice, and fine weather down the Beardmore to the Ross Ice Shelf.

But suddenly the capricious weather at the South Pole had closed in, and the Otter could not make the added height to get above the clouds heavy with ice. At two P.M. John Lewis decided to turn back to South Ice. He landed there at half past five in the evening.

This had an unforeseen consequence—one that utterly bewildered Admiral Dufek and his senior officers, so used to the careful preparations and abundant supplies with which all American sorties were planned. By making this abortive flight, Lewis had used up seven hours' worth of aviation fuel. When he returned to South Ice, he then discovered he didn't have enough fuel at the Depot to make a fresh attempt at the flight. There was extra fuel at Shackleton, but Lewis could not fly to Shackleton to fetch it, because the load would be so heavy. He would have had to make several trips merely to build up sufficient stock at South Ice to try again. It seemed crazy, as Dufek said, to leave such a small store of fuel at South Ice. However, the Americans helped, and willingly agreed to ferry some fuel and drop it at South Ice for Lewis, who was to make the attempt, this time successfully, later on.

Hillary was in difficulties too. The hard *sastrugi* of the Polar plateau had given way to soft snow, most unsuitable for the light Ferguson tractors. His fast daily average of around fifty miles a day had ended as deep snow repeatedly brought his tractors to a halt.

Speaking to his base, Hillary admitted, "At one time it appeared as if the tractor train had reached the end of the road. Deep bottom snow proved too much for the tractors and they bogged down again and again." Hillary had already pondered about reducing his load, and now he decided to do so. On the snow beside his tracks, the small party in bitter cold made a depot of every item they could spare from their food and fuel. They left behind two of their cargo sledges and more than a ton of supplies, reducing their rations and fuel to just the bare minimum necessary for the last hundred miles to the Pole.

During the night before, the tractors had been biting more than two feet into thick, soft snow. The team had spent hours clearing the tracks with shovels, but with the lighter load, the Fergusons were able to move forward again, though very slowly, and in low gear.

"Our main worry is fuel, but we are holding our own," reported Hillary, who had left Depot 700 with twenty drums of fuel, but had now only four drums left for the final dash.

Meanwhile, we waited—and waited—and waited. During the time of waiting, as I became more and more an old inhabitant of the Pole station, we pursued the time-honored pastime of Antarctica, trying to devise means of passing the hours. Admiral Byrd once remarked that the greatest problem was just trying to make the days pass. The scientific personnel had their work to do, but this could not possibly occupy all their waking hours. Conditions were too severe to permit continued working outside on the varied scientific tasks. They had to be done in spurts.

On New Year's Day, Vern had a great idea. We would have a picnic, outside on the ice. The notion was received with mixed feelings, but according to my diary, dated January 1:

"Last night we saw the old year out with a wild evening of Bourbon whisky and a double feature program on the cinema. Mogy came to the party in his pyjamas, saying it was easier thus to roll into bed when the festivities were over. We stayed up until about four in the morning, and today we started the New Year with an open air picnic. Temperature, minus twenty-two. We lit a fire—which bored its way down in the snow with astonishing ferocity until finally it was five feet below the surface—and fastened forks to the ends of long split bamboos. We used these to heat hot dogs over the fire, but the party was only a partial success. All the beer froze in ten minutes so we had nothing to drink. Finally, even the mustard froze, and the rolls in which the hot dog sausages were supposed to be put were eatable at the beginning, but after that they too became so hard you could hardly bite into them.

"Somebody had the bright idea of serving ice cream, but that too turned out to be a fiasco. We had no implements tough enough to cut the ice cream into reasonable portions, so most of it was left. We tried to warm it over the fire, but the carton caught fire yet the ice cream refused to melt. We stayed out for half an hour or so, eating the sausages off the long forks, then went in with sighs of relief, and I spent the afternoon of the first day of the year in bed."

This was only one of the many ways in which we tried to cheat time. I, personally, found that keeping a diary helped considerably in combating boredom, and now, I may say, helps considerably to refresh my mind about unimportant items that might otherwise have been forgotten. For instance, my first shower. On January 3, obviously for want of something better to do, I made a long entry into my Polar "log":

"Yesterday I had my first shower in Polar fashion. The rules are strict. You turn the shower on for fifteen seconds, turn it off while you soap yourself, rinse off for another fifteen seconds—and that does you for a fortnight.

"Today, I helped to roll barrels of oil, that had been parachuted, into the corridors—about the most pooping job I have ever done at this altitude. Now they are lining the tunnels, the only place where they can be easily available when the winter comes, for when the temperature really drops not only can a man's face freeze up in fifteen seconds, but the oil itself could turn like curdled milk. I have seen many strange brown patches of shredded material lying in the snow. I thought it was mashed up corrugated paper. It was oil, where a drum burst when being parachuted and froze up. Outside the huts stand the tractors. Sometimes some of them are not used for day after day, yet the engines are never stopped. They go on puffing away, just turning over, because if once they were stopped, who knows if ever they could be started again?

"We have another really serious problem here, too—garbage disposal. No system of sewage could possibly work well in this climate. You cannot pipe away unwanted liquids such as those from the toilets because they would freeze immediately they left the comparative warmth of the huts or corridors. So we have bulldozed big pits which when nearly filled with refuse—both human and otherwise—are snowed over and so keep the base clean. But now the winter is coming, it will soon be too cold even to walk out to the garbage pit. We are instead bulldozing a new pit twenty feet deep and nearly a hundred yards long, which will be covered over and connected to the camp by a tunnel. It is the only way the men can be sure that the waste products from the kitchen and the toilets can ever be taken out. There is no smell problem because everything freezes immediately. Already this garbage pit, though only twenty feet below the surface, has a steady temperature of minus forty.

"Nothing is more irritating here than to read in magazines of the Pole station being, as I recently read, 'a small, self-contained town with all modern conveniences.' It is true that we eat as much as we want, though the diet cannot be described as varied, and it is true that there is always a pot of coffee on the galley stove and a loaf of bread and a tin of peanut butter for snacks between meals, but these (and the ubiquitous films) must be put into perspective against the miseries that no cheerfulness can totally conceal—the lack of water for washing, the sleepless nights, getting out of bed each morning and poking a head out of the hut door into a blinding brilliance that leaves one sightless; the eternal business of putting clothes on and taking them off, the eternal fear of losing a glove or a scarf. Life is a perpetual snuffle and the stuff that causes the snuffle is forever making icicles hanging from one's nose. I came in the other day and literally had to snap one off. For myself, I have found it hardest of all here to bother to keep clean or tidy. Since the used water of the washroom cannot be drained, it is kept in a tank under the tin washbowl until full, then dumped. As I am apt to cough and splutter each morning at home anyway, I find it almost unbearable to wash my teeth over this mixture of everybody's leavings. The fact that the toilets are within a few feet doesn't help matters, for they have no water of course, they are just pits dug into the snow, with primitive seats made over them and are quite public. Each morning before I arise, I decide manfully to change my underclothes, but the effort of finding them in my kitbag while I am still in my sleeping bag has so far been beyond my courage. Each morning I make my bed in the corner of the hut where I am living. That means laying out my sleeping bag neatly. I do not, as my mother taught me, have to fold up my pyjamas, for I sleep in my underclothes, and if the night is unduly sharp, my shirt as well. I have managed to get an old packing case and make this into a sort of screen-with-dressing-table between my bed and the next one. Here I have a stock of cigarettes, my papers, different kinds of gloves for different kinds of excursions, and the vital tubes of grease for my lips. My family photos stand on the top—Titina, looking beautiful but a trifle severe, Bengy sucking a lollipop, and Sominetta just looking indescribably beautiful. Across the top of my camp bed I have strung a line of old parachute cord, on which over my head as I sleep dangle my socks, for they seem to get wet every day and I usually wear four pairs each time I go out for a longish walk.

"For extra warmth I scrounged an old silk parachute for a bed-cover. This is very gay in blue and red, but I noticed after the first night that it seemed very heavy for such a light material. I did nothing for several mornings—one always procrastinates here—but eventually I discovered that in its bulky folds which I had never quite disentangled there was enough snow to fill at least six buckets. It showed no signs of melting, so I have left it there."

Out on the trail, in the white wilderness, the two teams stumbled on. John Lewis at South Ice prepared for another try in his flight from South Ice to Scott, but had to wait for his petrol. Fuchs was still snowbound. By the evening of January 2, the temperature was minus twenty-eight degrees. The thermometer was dropping every day. That night the New Zealand tractor train moved forward another twenty-two miles. Hillary was nearly there.

9. *Sir Edmund Hillary Arrives at the South Pole*

It was ten minutes past one on the afternoon of Saturday, January 4, when Hillary reached the Pole. The time is one that historians should note because, as so often happens from remote places, differing reports were circulated in the world's Press. *The Times* and Reuter were still employing the temporary services of a New Zealand journalist who, though he was attached to Hillary, and had indeed spent fourteen days on the trail with him as far as Depot 700, for some reason refused an American invitation to fly to the Pole with me to meet his fellow countryman in his hour of triumph. Since I was the only British reporter at the Pole (together with three Americans by now), the other newspapers in England had perforce to rely on information from Scott Base. From the comfortable seclusion of this New Zealand base, so far from the South Pole, a completely inaccurate report was sent of the time of Hillary's arrival, many hours before he did in fact arrive. It was not, of course, deliberate; such an error is quite understandable when reporting momentous events from such a distance.

For two nights the Pole station had kept watch for the black dots on the horizon that would tell us of the approach of the tractor train. On Saturday morning, Mogy, using powerful binoculars, first sighted them. The moment was at hand. We all dressed up in our furs and parkas and almost the entire station trooped out to the ring of barrels that marked the actual site of the Pole.

It seemed hours until the tiny dots became real, moving objects. We debated what we should offer the Pole conqueror for lunch, finally deciding on sausages and beans because they would not spoil if left on the stove longer than was strictly necessary. By midday, the tractor train was clearly visible with the naked eye. It was a beautiful morning as the three vehicles came closer and closer. Eventually, Vernon and Mogy, as joint leaders, drove out in a Weasel to welcome them officially a mile or so from the Pole. They did not "escort" them in, preferring just to shake hands and offer them the hospitality of the Base; then Vernon, who was driving the Weasel, sheered off at right angles from Hillary's machines, and came back by a circuitous route, so that nobody could ever say Hillary had not come in on his own. A very pleasing gesture, I thought.

Yet, when the great moment arrived, it passed off almost without drama. The three crazy-looking tractors, roped to their sledges, suddenly became almost lifesize, then larger than lifesize. At first we could see no faces inside the makeshift canvas "tents" that had been rigged up to protect the drivers from the cold. Then the top of the leading Ferguson's cover was thrown back and up stood that amiable giant Ed Hillary and waved a greeting. The cameras without which no American is ever properly dressed clicked like mad. It was a glorious moment, a supreme moment. Hillary, looking bedraggled and dirty and with long, unkempt hair, jumped out on to the hard snow and we crowded round and shook him by the hand. It was the end of a long, long trail.

In the manner of modern life, the historic moment had to be relived several times for the photographers. The "original" handshake had to be performed over and over again, and then the grimy but grinning team assembled, and moved into closer formation so that all could perpetuate the moment.

"We look a fine bunch of men!" cried Hillary. All five men were bearded and bedraggled, with their coats and parkas torn, but they all gave great smiles as we walked from the Pole itself to the station, and all sat down for lunch, and handed out the letters for the expedition members which had arrived on the plane that took me to the Pole.

Actually, Hillary could have reached the Pole a day earlier had he wanted to, for he arrived within twenty miles of the Pole during the previous day, but decided to camp the night.

"I knew there would be a lot of fuss when we arrived," he grinned, "so as we had been driving twenty-four hours nonstop I thought we'd better prepare ourselves for the ordeal."

This was Hillary's great moment of personal triumph, and it was a likeable cheerful Hillary who came into our Press hut for a long talk, and his first beer for three months.

I was to get to know him very well. He was far more temperamental than one would suppose. There was none of the ice-cold efficiency of Fuchs, nor the suaveness. Standing six feet four, with his craggy head and big shoulders, it was impossible not to be immediately drawn to him. He had great charm. He was no braggart, but he was not politely overmodest, and certainly realised, in a quite charming way, the importance of being a hero, and its value in life. I felt before I left Antarctica even more sure that Hillary had all along planned this dash to the South Pole, as part of his perfectly legitimate "way of life" and would have been very upset if all the honors had gone to Fuchs and none to him. But this was in no way an unpleasant trait in his character. A hard-headed New Zealander, on whom the world's honors had fallen after Everest, he had a natural shyness and pleasant manner (when he wanted to exercise it) that made people enjoy his company, and I am sure that though he genuinely was bored with much of the social life inevitable in such conditions, he took a pleasure in the fact that his accomplishments singled him out as one of the greatest living adventurers. It would have been silly to think otherwise. Hillary was and is a man of enormous physical stature, with a heart and courage as great as his body. He wanted to get to the Pole.

But it was his magnificent physique that made him such a tackler of obstacles. The ordinary things of life were not enough for him; he was just too strong for them. Dr. Griffith Pugh, who was on Everest with him (and later came to greet Fuchs at the Pole) told me that the most remarkable thing about Hillary's fierce, explosive energy was his lung capacity. He calculated that Hillary's lungs were two liters superior to those of the average athlete. It was this which gave him his phenomenal stamina and endurance.

That afternoon, and the two following days in which we lived together at the Pole before flying back to McMurdo, Ed—he hated to be called Sir Edmund—and the other expedition members pieced together for me the first complete picture of what this historic dash had meant in hardship, danger, and (perhaps worst of all) boredom for its five members, each of whom had made part of the trip, though Hillary was the only one of the five who had made the complete journey from Scott to the Pole. The other four had only made sections of the journey, with substitutions for various reasons along the route. But they were all fine boys, every one of them; and even though (because of a communications problem) I had some slight difference of opinion with one of them, Hillary's radio man Peter Mulgrew, that had nothing to do with the fact that I had as great an admiration for Peter (and secret envy of his exploits) as the other members of the team. Each one of them did a truly heroic trek.

The most fantastic aspect of the whole journey was that when Hillary arrived, he had only enough gasoline left for another fifteen miles. It was almost incredible, but a most revealing insight into Hillary's character. He threw overboard all the rest of his fuel, took a calculated risk, knowing that if he had not done so, the weight of his equipment might easily have prevented him from completing the journey, which would have meant a rescue by air. In other words—failure. But Hillary was so determined to get to the Pole that he threw everything he didn't need away on the trail, and reached it with the ridiculously small margin of thirty gallons of gasoline to spare and enough food for perhaps another two weeks.

Equally fascinating was the fact that the trek of 1,300 miles, taking three months, had been made on ordinary farm tractors that anybody could buy. For three gruelling months in the worst weather in the world, the tractors had never given any serious trouble.

"If you overhaul them, they could go right back again," said Hillary as we sat on the edge of a bed, drinking canned beer, talking and yarning under the naked electric light bulbs, with a small Christmas tree still standing in a corner on a box of canned orange juice.

For a long time we sat there, other members of the expedition joining us and chiming in with their accounts of the exploit. But most of the story came from Hillary himself, and I can do no better than give it in his own words. If at times they seem a little disjointed, it is because I have refrained from changing them. They are as he spoke them as we sat in the hut, and drank beer while I made notes.

"We travelled by night," he began, "so as to navigate by the sun directly in front of us and we became quite attached to the old sun. Each day was exactly the same as the last. There have been no major hitches, but thank God it is over. The last 100 miles were not dangerous, but damned boring. That's the main trouble—it's so damned monotonous. All the way up here we saw only two sights —a lonely skua seagull 600 miles from the Pole, and one mountain 150 miles away.

"Some of us read books while sitting in the tractors because only one tractor needed to be navigated as they were roped together. The others followed in its tracks and their drivers were either reading or even sometimes dozing. In fact one of our biggest hardships was when our library ran out.

"The tractors, of course, were fantastic. We were skeptical at first, but they have been flat out for three months at between three and five miles an hour and in soft snow we could only travel in bottom or second gear. Even then it was touch and go whether the gasoline would last out for the final hundred miles; but as a result of this I believe it is now possible for the Americans to set up a regular tractor train route between McMurdo and the Pole.

"We didn't have too much trouble with crevasses. When their presence was suspected, two people were sent ahead roped together to discover bridges over the crevasses. The deepest crevasse looked literally bottomless.

"The best moment of the trip was at Christmas when we drank our bottle of Scotch, and the New Zealand radio put on a special program for us. Our biggest thrill was when we nearly lost one tractor in a crevasse, but fortunately the other two were able to haul it out. But crevasses weren't really our biggest problem— our biggest trouble started when we began crossing the Polar plateau, putting up our tents in twenty-five-mile-an-hour winds. The lowest temperature we encountered was minus forty-one degrees" (which with a twenty-five-mile-an-hour wind would equal a temperature on the body of minus sixty-six).

Hillary told me that for three months he had never taken off his underclothes and had never had a real wash. "We slept an average of six hours out of each twenty-four," he added, "and had our biggest meal at eight every morning."

Members of the party gave me their daily on-the-trail routine: starting with oatmeal for breakfast at five P.M. (remember, they travelled by night), then six hours of driving, after which a forty-five minute break for cocoa and biscuits, another six hours on the tractor, and dinner at eight A.M. Some of the men ate (and even liked) pemmican, but Hillary's main diet was his favorite bacon and powdered eggs.

"If anybody ever offers me eggs again, I'll kill them!" groaned Derek Wright, the team's photographer.

They carried no fresh or frozen meat. Some was flown out on one occasion by John Claydon, but something had gone wrong and it had to be thrown away. And throughout the entire trip, they never drank tea. Only cocoa—"thick and sweet," said Hillary.

I asked Hillary two forthright questions. The first was "Why did you come to the Pole?"

"Because I wanted to," answered Hillary, adding with a grin, "Some people have to have a scientific reason. Not me."

"Is there any friction between you and Fuchs because of this dash of yours?"

"Bunny wished us luck," replied Hillary. "We expected he might be here first."

It was inevitable that we should talk about Fuchs, who was far behind schedule, with almost 1,500 miles to go and the prospect of howling blizzards on the plateau as winter came nearer. Despite previous optimistic reports, Fuchs, at the moment when the world focus was centered on Hillary, was still many miles from the Pole and halted again by a whiteout. I never did understand that remark "We expected he might be here first." It was quite obvious that, even without the scientific work which slowed down Fuchs so much, his heavier caravan could never travel at a speed equal to Hillary's lightweight team. Hillary, already rather despondent about the prospect of wintering over, told me flatly, "Fuchs may be many weeks getting here. Let's hope he makes it before the winter. But I don't want to stay. Not me, old boy. One winter here is enough. My future plans are to get home to New Zealand and look after my family. It's time we returned to the children."

On the first night, after the expedition members had read their letters, the first for many weeks, we had a big party. The champagne had already been drunk at Christmas, but we had a "happy hour" with Old Methusalem bourbon, from which Vernon made American old fashioned cocktails which normally include bitters, orange, and cherry. Due to the lack of fresh fruit, he evolved his own old fashioneds, by sweetening the bourbon with cherry-flavoured sweets and letting the mixture stand two weeks before serving over snow. We dined off meat loaf, beans, corn, potato, and pumpkin pie.

"I'll have to watch my manners now," said one of the New Zealanders, "I'm so used to eating while lying down in my sleeping bag, I've almost forgotten how to use knives and forks at a table."

Hillary himself, twenty pounds lighter, grunted, "I just can't eat it all." We all saw a film after dinner. Because he was so used to travelling by night, neither Hillary nor any expedition members were sleepy when the normal bedtime arrived. We sat and yarned in the cozy living room I had come to know so well, and it was then that Hillary decided he would fly out when I did on January 7th. He planned to take four of the team with him, leaving Mulgrew, the radio operator, at the Pole to deal with messages from Fuchs. Fuchs was so obviously going to take weeks to reach the Pole there was no point in my remaining there. Also I had more photographs, and some hope that for the first time it would be possible to radio out pictures I had taken of Hillary's arrival at the Pole. McMurdo was trying to lay it on. It meant transmitting the photographs by radio to New York, then retransmitting them by radio-telephone to London. It was worth a shot.

That being decided, and praying for good flying weather, we all turned in, most of the expedition members sleeping in the South Pole Press Hut, their first night on a bed for many a long week.

Hillary needed a good sleep on that great night—for within a few hours of his arrival at the Pole, the storm of controversy burst open and the world was starting to buzz with the question that will never be satisfactorily answered: "Should he have gone on to the Pole?" There were some who felt, and still do feel strongly, that he let Fuchs down, that this was "Fuchs' show" and that Hillary's job was to stay at Depot 700, however late Fuchs was for his appointment in the white desert.

There is one important point that was never really dwelt upon, but which made all the difference in assessing Hillary's actions. Did Hillary decide to go to the Pole *after* reaching Depot 700, or long, long before? We know that he did not discuss the Pole dash with Fuchs until Depot 700 was properly established, at which time

Hillary knew how far away Fuchs was. But did Hillary refrain from asking Fuchs for permission until then—yet having had the secret idea all through the expedition that he would get to the Pole before Fuchs if it were possible? It is one thing to arrive at a lonely spot in the Antarctic, do your job, find yourself with a month on your hands, and then on the spur of the moment, decide to go for the Pole. It is another to have agreed to wait for the expedition leader at a given point, knowing all the time that, if humanly possible, you would try to get to the Pole.

I believe that this was no sudden decision of Hillary's. I believe he had his dream of reaching the Pole for more than a year. I am convinced that right from the time he agreed to be assistant to Fuchs, Hillary hoped that he would reach the Pole. I do not for a moment suggest he would have disobeyed any instruction if Fuchs had been on time at 700. Hillary might then have been a disappointed man, with very little of the glory that has been showered on the expedition.

The Times, in a leading article, described Ed Hillary's trek to the Pole as "a personal and unpremeditated sally to the Pole." But was it? All the evidence points to the contrary.

Hillary himself said that "I came to the Pole because I wanted to come to the Pole. Some people have to have a scientific reason. Not me." To this he added the categorical statement, "I have harbored the idea of a Pole trip for nearly a year," adding perhaps the most significant phrase of the whole dispute, "But I don't believe in calling my shots in advance."

That seems to me to indicate perfectly clearly that Hillary had nurtured the Pole dream in secret.

The whole of Hillary's dash to the Pole contained many strange sidelights. Consider these. When Sir Edmund Hillary was at Depot 700, he told Dr. Fuchs that he would "scrub the Pole jaunt"—abandon his plans—if he could help Dr. Fuchs in any way. He also told me that Fuchs had wished him luck on his trip to the Pole.

But there was a way in which Hillary could have further helped Fuchs, and that was by laying another depot.

When Hillary reached Depot 700, he spent ten days preparing the depot for Dr. Fuchs, and he then asked Fuchs (according to Hillary himself) whether there was anything else he could do. Hillary told Fuchs at this time that he proposed "venturing another 200 miles southward to find a way for the Fuchs party through the crevasses and *possibly* to push on to the Pole."

So Hillary set off southward. A day's journey out of 700, he managed to contact Fuchs, but not personally, saying he had left 700 to prove the route for two hundred miles. He told Fuchs he would go out one hundred miles while waiting Fuchs' reply, and offered to abandon any journey to the Pole if he could help. To this Hillary received a reply from Fuchs saying he was delighted Hillary was marking the trail south of 700, but the cable from Fuchs did not mention the Pole at all. Hillary waited a day when one hundred miles towards the Pole, but no other message came from Fuchs. Four days out from Depot 700, Hillary pushed on another hundred miles. He was now three hundred miles from the Pole. The going was easy. He had cleared the crevassed areas.

Now comes another mystery. When Hillary was 260 miles from Depot 700—virtually half way to the Pole—he at last received a cable from Fuchs. This cable asked Hillary to establish a further depot at 800, to be laid as a precaution. This depot, which Hillary never laid, was 160 miles behind him, and 240 miles from the Pole. Yet Hillary told me that by the time the message reached him, he was beyond the point of no return. Return to where?

The answer doesn't make sense. Without doing anything more than turning round, Hillary could have pursued one of two courses:

He could have returned to Depot 700, the same distance as the Pole from the point where he received the message. If he had enough fuel and food to reach the Pole, he had enough to return to 700. There the fuel he had used up on the Pole dash could easily have been replaced by air, the cargo being flown in by John Claydon, waiting with his aircraft for just such orders as these. Hillary could then have laid Depot 800.

Or—he could have gone back to a point one hundred miles south of Depot 700, and laid out Depot 800.

Did he have enough food to hang on and lay a depot at 800? He certainly did have enough food and fuel to go to 800 and make preliminary plans for laying the depot because, as Hillary himself told me, he jettisoned nearly a ton of fuel and food on the trail in order to lighten his vehicles for the last dash to the Pole.

Could he not have used that food and fuel to start a base at 800? Or else have gone back to 700, and find Claydon there awaiting him, with the necessary supplies to lay 800?

The whole business of the nonexistent Depot 800 was extremely mysterious. Why did Fuchs ask for this depot? Fuchs above all men is an ice-cold, highly efficient explorer who had planned with meticulous care for months ahead. As he proved by his last magnificent run home to Scott Base, his bases from 700 down to Scott were chosen with mathematical precision and could not have been better placed. The expedition never had any need for an extra depot at 800. Is it not an odd fact that Fuchs, the master planner of the expedition, suddenly changed all his ideas of where the bases should be, and after Hillary's request to proceed to the Pole, asked Hillary to lay another depot for him? That cable was delayed for four days—unaccountably. Was it Fuch's polite way of trying to stop Hillary from reaching the Pole before him? And was Hillary's remark about "the point of no return" his polite way of saying that the Pole came first?

It is perhaps therefore not inopportune to note that Fuchs and Hillary did not like each other. That is the truth. My colleague T. F. Thompson, who was with the expedition in its early stages on the Weddell Sea, observed this too. He mentioned it at the time of the disagreement in an open letter to Hillary:

"Bunny was delighted when you agreed to lead the support

group which would establish the food and fuel depots and finally lead the crossing party to safety at Scott Base. There was no thought of glory for himself nor of keeping New Zealand out of the picture. As token of this he took your close friend and fellow countryman George Lowe on the crossing party.

"Unfortunately it now seems a new factor came into the picture. Yourself and Bunny, each of you a splendid bloke, did not exactly hit it off together. When I met your ship after you had jointly established the advance party on the Weddell Sea coast, it was one story I did not write. I had hoped never to write it. For it was then obvious from little incidents and little hints dropped that the temperaments of the two leaders clashed. I noticed that you and Dr. Fuchs never voluntarily got together. But I always hoped that what was below the surface would never come into view—certainly never result in an open break in the full glare of world publicity."

Well—now Ed Hillary was at the Pole. What next? There were three courses open to him—to wait for Fuchs at the Pole, and thus help him with the Polar plateau crossing; to take his tractor back to 700 (the Americans having offered him sufficient fuel and food) and wait there as originally planned; or to fly from the Pole back to Scott Base, and pass the interim time in the comfort that this real base afforded.

After three months on the trail, nobody can blame Hillary for deciding to return to Scott Base, as he would naturally fly up to meet Fuchs when he arrived at 700. But was it the right decision? It might have been—after all, Hillary's job was to meet Fuchs at Depot 700 and escort him down the glacier. It might have been—except for one extraordinary thing that happened at the Pole, while we were all there, but of which we knew nothing at the time.

For while Hillary was basking in world fame—as Fuchs was struggling in a whiteout—while Hillary was deciding to fly back to Scott Base, he talked on the radio, in secret, to Dr. Fuchs, still so many miles away.

The details of that talk would never have been made public

except for a piece of sheer bad luck, but that talk contained one question from Fuchs—and one answer from Hillary.

Fuchs asked him—if not in these words—"Now that you have got to the Pole, will you hang on at the Pole till I get there and escort me back across the plateau?"

Hillary refused.

10. Conflict Between Fuchs and Hillary

ED HILLARY and I flew back to McMurdo on January 6th. I had been at the Pole for about two weeks and, due to communications difficulties, was out of touch with my office. So it was that I did not know until two days later of the private telegrams exchanged between Fuchs and Hillary which were to result in the open row between the two men—private messages made public in error.

Before I knew about them, Hillary and I had a long talk at Scott Base, where we had a cup of real English tea and talked for an hour.

"Bunny is chugging along to the Pole and making about thirty miles a day," said Hillary. "I would say that he can maintain an average of thirty miles a day all the way home. He told me he expected to be at the Pole on January 17, and at this rate it will take him another forty-five days to reach Scott Base."

We poured out more tea, and Hillary added significantly, "That is, if the weather holds. On the other hand, it's getting late in the season and there is a chance of bad weather for vehicles that have already had a severe thrashing. The temperature on the plateau is much lower in February than in January. Naturally I

hope we won't have to winter over for a second time, and I'm sure
Bunny's party thinks the same. But if anybody winters over, it's
better it should be Bunny's party and so most of us will go home
before winter. I of course will have to stay if necessary. I have no
alternative."

As he was telling me this, the whole row had blown up
across the pages of the world's newspapers, due to what the New
Zealanders described as "a series of tragicomic errors." Hillary
had sent a cable suggesting Fuchs stop at the Pole. It was addressed
to the London Committee of the expedition, but a copy was sent
to Mr. Charles Bowden, of the Ross Sea Committee. Bowden's
copy became mixed up with a number of press messages and
was broadcast over the New Zealand radio.

From that moment the row was on, for Hillary's message
was the one that caused poor Fuchs, so hard pressed, to cry back
to Hillary, in effect, "We don't need you. We'll get through by
ourselves."

Hillary's message was sent to Marshal of the RAF Sir John
Slessor, chairman of the London Committee of Management. It
read in full:

"Fuchs on Sunday morning January 5th was 357 miles from
the Pole in heavy *sastrugi* (snow ridges) and doing repairs to a
Weasel. He advises that the Otter reported a very high ridge
covered with enormous *sastrugi* at about 87 degrees South.
Although he hoped, with reasonable luck, to be at the Pole by
January 20, this will require a much higher average than he has
been able to maintain.

"Have expressed my views to Fuchs that with extreme delay
in his programme and the punishment his vehicles are sustaining
he would be most unwise to attempt to continue on over the
1,250 miles to Scott Base this season. This journey could only be
done at considerable risk to men and at the sacrifice of any effect-
ive seismic program. I suggested that he winter his vehicles at the
South Pole, that his party be evacuated by air, and that in November they fly in again to the Pole in ample time to recondition

their vehicles and complete their journey with full scientific progress.

"I have no doubt that Admiral Dufek would be anxious to assist in this as Fuchs does not realise that his delayed progress is causing considerable concern, not only to ourselves but also to the Americans. They accept the fact that it will be their job, whether they are asked or not, to initiate rescue action and that, therefore, both naval and air forces will be tied up here awaiting Fuchs' safe arrival.

"Although Fuchs requested that one of my mechanics accompany him from the Pole to Scott Base, neither of my men, who have done an outstanding job, is prepared to take on this job, which they regard as extremely foolhardy at this time of year. When I advised Fuchs of my views he replied more in sorrow than in anger and expressed himself determined to go despite all.

"Although Fuchs was anxious for me to travel with him from the Pole, I have advised him, rather than wait several weeks inactively at the Pole, I would return to Scott Base and get on with my job and then join him at one of the depots. To my mind, enough prestige will have been gained by the arrival of Fuchs and ourselves at the South Pole to enable a modification of the plan to allow the task to be carried out in a reasonable and safe manner over a two-year period, whereas a forced march late in the season could well cause both unfavourable publicity. Your instructions are the only thing that can enable Fuchs to save face and adopt a modified plan, so I would earnestly request that the management committee should give this matter its earliest consideration."

This was an incredible message! Hillary had of course every right to offer advice, but in what terms he made it! Could we really talk about a man like Fuchs "saving face." Why, it is the last thing Fuchs would ever care about, he was far above that sort of thing! Fuchs was a man who, despite any faults, was completely honest with himself. He would never have been influenced by "saving face."

But this was nothing, absolutely nothing, compared with the real truth that came out of the telegrams—that Hillary had refused to wait at the Pole for Fuchs. No wonder that Sir Miles Clifford, a former Governor of the Falkland Islands, and a member of the British Trans-Antarctic Committee, said: "I know Hillary well and he is the last man I would expect to have a swollen head or be silly. I am sure it (his decision to fly from the Pole) is all a mistake. I find it absolutely incredible."

And no wonder that Fuchs, on being acquainted with this extraordinary outburst, replied to Sir John Slessor crisply: "Have received message from Hillary urging me to abandon journey at Pole, and return there next season to continue work. His grounds are deterioration of weather late in the season. I am aware of this possibility which must be accepted. I have informed him that there is no question of abandonment, and return of party following season is impracticable.

"He does not wish to accompany us from Pole, but offers to join us at Depot 700. He states his agreement with his mechanics' view that continuation of the journey late in the season is an unjustifiable risk. I do not agree, but have informed him that I do not feel able to ask him to join us at Depot 700 to use his local knowledge but will find our own way out."

What a heart cry from Fuchs! To me, the most important point was not the difference of opinion between two men, each entitled to his own opinion, but the clear truth, emerging from the cables, that Hillary had refused Fuchs' request that he should remain at the Pole. This refusal—in Fuchs' words, "He did not wish to accompany us from the Pole"—was I think unforgivable on the part of Hillary. It nearly brought disaster to the expedition, and as Mr. T. F. Thompson, part of whose letter to Hillary I have quoted, wrote, "Now relations have deteriorated so much that Bunny Fuchs, on the verge of exhaustion as he leads his team through sheer frozen hell, cables 'We don't want Sir Edmund to meet us at Depot 700. We can do without his local knowledge and find our own way down the glacier.' That is a heart cry of a man who thinks himself betrayed, and the tragic thing is that he and his party do need your help and badly. . . . On the face of it, my inclination at the moment is to say: 'Poor show, Sir Edmund. Poor show.' "

Slessor immediately cabled Fuchs, "The Committee have considered your telegram and Hillary's. We have full confidence in you and your judgment as leader of the expedition. We support your decision and any other you may make. Best wishes and congratulations on present progress."

Why did Hillary do it? Why, having reached the Pole, did he not at least stay there for two weeks, in comparative comfort? Had Hillary stayed on at the Pole, even his bitterest critics would have had to admit that his courage had aided Fuchs, because he would then have used his spare time to guide Fuchs across another five hundred miles of snow and ice, and thus hasten his progress. With Hillary in the leading Sno-Cat, Fuchs would have made better time, and Hillary's Polar dash would have been hailed as a courageous venture to aid the other hard-pressed explorers, by providing them with invaluable guidance for an extra five hundred miles between the Pole and Depot 700.

But Hillary said no, adding that he would return to Scott Base "and get on with my job." What job? I saw Hillary "doing his job" at Scott Base.

He was chipping ice with a spade in one of the corridors.

Rear-Admiral Parry, secretary of the Expedition, carefully pointed out that the disagreement between the two men "was not a quarrel but merely a difference of opinion," but I am much more intrigued by the guarded reply that Slessor, when interviewed on the BBC, made, when asked whether Hillary had sent his cable direct to the London headquarters with the idea that pressure should be brought to bear on Dr. Fuchs from London. Slessor said, "It might so appear."

Indeed it might.

In a leading article on January 9, *The Times*, in part, said that "the apparent disharmony between the two sections of the

Antarctic expedition has been overcome. Disagreement there has evidently been; if it ever approached the dimensions of a quarrel, judgment at long range was bound to start from the presumption that Dr. Fuchs was in the right. Sir Edmund Hillary, though a subordinate, has been properly entrusted with a large power of initiative. His individual thrust to the Pole was quite legitimate, for he had already done his duty by establishing . . . the depots provided for in the general plan."

The Times did not mention that Depot 800 was requested, but went on to add, "Not only Sir Edmund Hillary's personal honour, but the credit of New Zealand, is involved in the scrupulous performance of his duty to support Dr. Fuchs to the full extent of his power," then went on to say, "If there was ever any ground for interpreting his return by air from the Pole to Scott Base as a presage of withdrawal from the expedition, he [Hillary] has set doubts at rest."

But nobody ever suggested that Hillary was going to quit the expedition. Indeed, at the Pole, Hillary told me that he was most certainly prepared to winter over if necessary. I never received the slightest impression that Hillary would leave Bunny Fuchs in the lurch. His later public affirmation of what was already well known —that he would support Fuchs to the end—had no bearing on Hillary's decision not to stay at the Pole and wait for Bunny.

In London, the Expedition held day-long conferences over the crisis, and the same night that they cabled Fuchs they also cabled Mr. Bowden of the Ross Sea Committee, the New Zealander who had (perhaps for the best) inadvertently made these disagreeable points of view public. Slessor asked Bowden to tell Hillary to investigate the possibility of establishing more bases, in a cable which read:

"We believe Fuchs' progress across most difficult country thoroughly satisfactory and would now expect his rate of progress to increase substantially as indeed is happening.

"Should further delays through any reason occur, however,

then the duties of the supporting parties under Hillary become correspondingly greater.

"We consider these duties should include the laying of additional depots, including 800 should Fuchs so require, and would urge that the necessary action to this end be begun, using Otter as necessary.

"Most grateful for your valuable cooperation hitherto. Emphasize as previously that Hillary's primary job is to make as certain as humanly possible that Fuchs reaches Scott Base this season."

This depot was never laid, even though Fuchs later was to say to me, "We would perhaps have liked it."

Slessor's message, it will be noted, did not ask Hillary to lay a new depot, only to be ready to lay one "should Fuchs so require," and on January 9 Hillary, in a radio telephone talk to the New Zealand Press Association, said no request had been received from any quarter to establish a new depot for Dr. Fuchs—and he added the unfortunate phrase "I hope none will come." It would strain the resources of the New Zealand expedition to the utmost to establish Depot 800, though he did say, "But we'd give it a go."

The *Times* part-time correspondent summed up the "confused picture" in Antarctica on January 8, writing "The decision to ask Sir Edmund Hillary to report on plans for the establishment of Depot 800, which would be 800 miles from Scott Base, has added further confusion to an already confused picture of the Antarctic adventure. When Sir Edmund left Depot 700 and began moving farther south it was assumed at the London headquarters that he was complying with Dr. Fuchs' reported request that an additional depot be set up 100 miles farther on (Depot 800). But then came the New Zealander's quite unexpected 'hell-bent for the Pole' message and one might well ask now what useful purpose that journey served."

What indeed! But how useful it would have been if only Hillary had stayed on at the Pole. I believe that Hillary, though his personal courage was never in doubt, was not the ideal choice for a supporting role, a man like Dr. Fuchs. I do not think any other man in the world could have reached the Pole so quickly, for Hillary is not only a man of exceptional courage as well as exceptional endurance—but only while there is something to do. Now that the Pole dash was over, all Hillary could see was Fuchs wasting time on seismic soundings, while he was frankly dismayed at the prospect of possibly staying another winter in Antarctica, though quite prepared to do so.

At this time I myself was concerned as to whether Fuchs would make it. Indeed I cabled at some length of the grave difficulties facing Fuchs, doubtless influenced to a certain degree by my close association with Hillary, and in my diary of January 7 I wrote: "What are the chances of Fuchs winning out? They are getting slimmer every day and it might well be that Fuchs will have to take a chance as difficult as that which faced Shackleton—to call it off in the interests of his men. Fuchs is still around three hundred miles from the Pole and he can't possibly reach Scott Base before early March. By the end of February there will be no more flying. Hillary tells me flying will stop when the temperature reaches minus forty and it is going down every day. After the Pole, if Fuchs decides to go on, there will be almost no hope of picking him up if he gets into trouble as the New Zealand planes have not the range to reach him further south than 700."

I made some of these views apparent in a cable to the *Daily Mail*, but once I had seen the original cables between Fuchs and Hillary, and then talked to Fuchs at the Pole, I changed my mind completely. Now he *had* to go on.

It must not be thought that all the blame rests on Hillary. Fuchs is an explorer in the Scott tradition, aloof, well-mannered, completely uninterested in the passage of time. I thought it typical of his attitude to the outside world that he tried to have information blocked at the South Pole station which he was using so regularly. And later, when we met Fuchs at the Pole, I was told by his expedition members that during the quarrel between the two leaders, while half the world was clamouring that he should stop at the Pole, Fuchs never even discussed the question with his expedition members.

It is slightly bizarre to reflect that (if what the men told me is true), here you had these twelve men, many of whom had been through frightful ordeals for months, cut off from civilisation on the ice cap, while their leader was exchanging acrimonious messages with his subordinate, and keeping it "secret." But of course it was no secret. Fuchs, apparently, said nothing to his men, even though he must have been debating with himself whether or not he should call the expedition off at the Pole. But every member of the expedition knew all about the row, for they picked it up on the BBC. What a touch of the macabre, to think that the men on the trail had to receive information about their own welfare from the BBC in London!

I wrote in my diary at the time, "This trans-Antarctic adventure has received lop-sided publicity. I think that if a man like Fuchs wants to undertake such an adventure, helped by government funds, its activities should be much more a matter of common property. Hillary agrees with me. When I was with Hillary at the Pole, Hillary withheld nothing from me, and said, 'I disagree with this business of dealing with only one newspaper—ask me any questions you like.' "

And, as the *Daily Telegraph* said on January 11, "The Americans (in Antarctica) are willing to help Dr. Fuchs and have offered to fly him from the Pole. But they are puzzled by his apparent secrecy. Although he uses their South Pole facilities to relay messages to Scott Base, he is passing them in code and is even reluctant to give the Americans his position or possible date of arrival at the Pole."

As this quarrel gained publicity around the middle of January, how was Fuchs—dogged, determined Fuchs—progressing? By January 10, he had reached a point 230 miles from the Pole, after repeated setbacks which had tried him sorely. He had finally set off for the Pole from South Ice on Christmas Day, and hoped the journey would take seventeen days. Fuchs had sent one message some days previously announcing that because he was three weeks behind his original planned timing, "We shall be attempting long daily runs to catch up as much as possible. But the daily mileage will be controlled by the time needed for glaciological work and the seismic sounding of the ice depth."

All the same, once South Ice was behind him, Fuchs made extremely good time. He did not reach the Pole on the date he had hoped (he was three days late) but his journey was remarkable, and much more difficult than Hillary's "jaunt," for while Hillary was travelling light, Fuchs still had four Sno-Cats, three Weasels, and one Muskeg (later abandoned). These vehicles and their sledges were carrying thirty tons, of which twenty-one tons were gasoline. Ken Blaiklock and Jon Stephenson, in charge of the two dog teams (to be abandoned at the Pole) traveled ahead of the main party to mark danger areas directly in Fuchs' path.

During this journey, and during the unfortunate differences of opinion, there was one bright spot. John Lewis, of the RAF, finally managed to get his Otter plane to Scott Base. He had, as I have recounted, tried once before but had been forced to return to South Ice owing to bad weather. Now he achieved his ambition, a remarkable one, unhappily almost unnoticed during the flurry of undiplomatic exchanges between the better-known characters of the expedition. It was the first single-engined aircraft to cross the Antarctic continent.

While John was waiting at South Ice in bad weather for the Americans to fly in fuel, there was one small hut almost covered with snow. He and his crew of three—Flight Lieutenant Gordon Haslop, a New Zealander, and Sergeants Peter Weston and Ellis Williams of Britain—had to live in the hut for a week. The gasoline arrived. The Americans flew in five drums of fuel from Ellsworth Base in a Dakota. Then Lewis had to sit out the same whiteouts that were slowing up Bunny Fuchs on the trail.

On January 6, the weather cleared, and at 11:52 A.M. the party of four set off from South Ice. Two hours later, they dipped their wings over Dr. Fuchs, on the trail below. They saw the South Pole Station, though ice crystals formed a bad haze, at 4:28 P.M. and flew directly over the station. This time the weather was good all the way. Lewis told me that though there was cloud over the Pole plateau, he was always able to get above it, and the leg down the Beardmore Glacier was made in wonderful weather, with the winds helping the tiny single-engined aircraft all the way home. He landed at Scott Base at 10:49 P.M. in vivid sunlight, having taken 10 hours 57 minutes for the 1,250 miles air distance from South Ice. His remarkable flight received almost no public acclaim, but as *The Times* said, "It was a brave journey; and it stands among the many brave journeys which now interlace Antarctica."

As the days passed, Fuchs made better and better time and soon I had to decide whether or not to fly up to the Pole again (if it were possible) to greet him. From the purely personal point of view, I was not particularly anxious to make the trip. The weather was bad, the flying conditions were getting worse day by day, and quite apart from any small risk involved in the actual flights, I was worried by the possibility that once there, I might have to spend many weeks at the Pole and not be able to get out.

My colleagues, who had by now started to catch up with me, were much of the same mind. I talked the matter over with Merle Macbain; the position was simple. If nobody particularly wanted to go, why go? We could have a voice conference with Fuchs when he reached the Pole, and the resultant dispatches would reach London much more quickly if filed from McMurdo. On the other hand, if one went, all went.

Jack Coley, in charge of all flying, said the weather was "lousy" and he didn't want to risk his neck. But we reckoned without the Admiral, who had twice been "in the drink" in Antarctica, and had managed to live despite several hair-raising aircraft accidents.

On the evening of January 16, he held a cocktail party— whisky and snow or gin and snow, take your pick—in the Admiral's hut. Hillary came along. We all had a few drinks, not many, but enough to make us a little more cheerful than usual, and suddenly found we had missed the camp dinner, served each evening at the ungodly hour of 5:30 P.M.

Admiral Dufek, who normally queued for his meals, asked the cookhouse to fill a large pan with spaghetti and meat balls, and this was brought over. We ate it off cardboard plates, and drank beer or coffee with it.

As the meal ended, Admiral Dufek suddenly rose, and holding his cup in the air, cried, "Gentlemen—to Ed and Bunny! And come along, gentlemen! Let's all fly up to the Pole—tomorrow if the weather's good—and see Bunny in."

That was that. The weather—there are some who might add, unfortunately—was good. Or good enough.

"Would Ed Hillary come?"

"Of course you'll come!" said Dufek, and that was also that.

We finished our scratch meal, grabbed another free drink each (by now alcohol was becoming very scarce at McMurdo) and went to our huts to pack. Hillary and Griffith Pugh, the Everest physiologist who was living in a tent near Scott Base, returned for their survival equipment. Very early the next morning, loaded like cattle on the floors of two Neptunes, we set off once again for the Pole.

On a beautiful sunny January morning we sighted the ring of drums. Admiral Dufek was in the other plane, and he radioed us to follow him; we would fly out over the cap and try and find Fuchs. We found him, thirty miles or so from the Pole. Our Neptune circled low, following the Admiral's, and we flew down to a hundred feet over the tiny straggling band of men and their vehicles.

The Admiral talked to him and Fuchs made it quite clear once again that he would push on from the Pole to Depot 700. When asked if there was anything the Americans could do to help, he answered, "It would be very nice if we could have a shower, and I would appreciate being able to stay two or three days for a thorough overhaul of my vehicles. And then straight on to finish the job."

We waved au revoir and turned around. Soon I was back at the Pole again with old friends; the two Neptunes flew off as Vernon Houk, debonair and cheerful as ever, came out to greet me. So did Mogy. That afternoon we all started into real hard work —and never was it performed with more genuine pleasure: digging snow so that there would be enough hot water for Bunny's showers when he arrived. They certainly needed them.

11. Dr. Vivian Fuchs Arrives at the South Pole

AT 1:15 on the afternoon of Monday, January 20, Bunny Fuchs led his Commonwealth Trans-Antarctic Expedition into the South Pole base. Flags flying, his leading tractor, Rock 'n Roll, ground to a halt, Fuchs jumped out, Hillary strode forward to meet him, and Fuchs said, "It's damn good to see you, Ed." Then he turned to Admiral Dufek, and commented, "It's a long way from our meeting in Paris, Admiral."

Behind Fuchs, the Sno-Cats slowly caught up and stopped in the snow, almost at the edge of the Polar base. The two yelping dog teams, with their drivers crying instructions, came alongside, and the huskies flopped in the snow.

It was a glorious morning, cold but sunny, as the caravan spilled out its grimy, tired men who had been driving the tractors almost daily since they left Shackleton Base on November 24.

For without doubt this first half of the journey was by far the most gruelling. Tractor trouble had caused delay after delay, particularly before South Ice which could, without any exaggeration, be called the worst terrain in the world.

As Fuchs said, "It is difficult to convey our practical problems and the almost incessant feeling of frustration, our movements restricted by weather or terrain or need to repair vehicles."

For eight weeks they had been travelling, sometimes at speeds of a mile or less an hour. Already the expedition had had to abandon four out of the nine vehicles with which they started out from Shackleton. Yet, throughout, Fuchs had kept stolidly on with his scientific work.

This was my first meeting with Fuchs and, as one might have expected, he was a tremendously impressive man, wearing bright red moccasins, a blue parka, a white roll-top sweater and a black peaked cap. He had no gloves over his blackened and calloused hands. His fine blond beard, streaked with grey, came neatly and naturally to a clean point. A very handsome man; he reminded me every inch of the captain of a ship. He said to Hillary, "I've a lot to talk to you about," but then, as Dufek led him into the base with Vernon and Mogy, Hillary went off to see his great chum George Lowe, the New Zealand member of the Fuchs team, who arrived wearing an enormous straw hat.

As with Hillary's arrival, there was a big welcoming committee. Everything had to be done several times "for the record": shaking hands, close-ups of Hillary and Fuchs, of the two explorers with the Admiral. Even the poor dogs had to be put into action again for the cameras.

We had first sighted the expedition soon after breakfast, and, after some hesitation, had decided to go out to meet them. We rigged up two Weasels, each pulling a sled, and crowded aboard. Off we went through fairly soft snow in a straight line towards the dots on the horizon. But they were much farther off than we realised. And also, Mogy, the scientific leader, had asked Fuchs to come in along a special route, carefully flagged to show the way along the last five miles into the Pole; this route was marked so that vehicles did not cross patches of terrain where scientific observations were being made. But this caused some delay, for Fuchs apparently picked up the wrong flag and had to change course. Admiral Dufek (to say nothing of the rest of us) was getting a little short-tempered with the cold which started biting into us after waiting for an hour.

So we all decided to go back, a complete anticlimax. We turned the Weasels round, and had an impromptu race back to the Pole, for miles across the snow. There we took off all our heavy clothing and made a beeline for the coffee pots. It was as well we did, for Fuchs took another three hours to reach us.

What good hosts the Americans make! Neither Fuchs nor Hillary wished to inconvenience the Pole, and indeed both had to be persuaded to accept warm beds after their gruelling weeks on the trail; Fuchs, almost the moment he arrived, asked "Where shall we pitch our tents?" But the Americans insisted. As soon as Houk knew that Fuchs needed a couple of days for repair work (which in theory Fuchs could have done with his portable equipment in the open) the Pole team cleared out their entire garage. All machines were taken into the open air, where incongruously they were left with their engines chugging away for three days to keep them warm! The garage empty, mechanics arranged in proper order all necessary equipment so that Fuchs' engineers could start work when they wanted.

We planned to leave the Pole within a few hours of Fuchs' arrival, to get photos of the meeting out of McMurdo. So that morning we cleaned up our hut, put in a new supply of beer (keeping it off the ground so that it would be unfrozen for the guests) and carted in extra beds for the team who used it for a couple of days. Since there was a great batch of mail awaiting Fuchs, Vernon emptied one of the sleeping bunks of all personal belongings, and turned this over to the doctor as his private "office" for the stay at the Pole.

Together Fuchs and Hillary had now conquered a continent of ice. First Hillary had reached the Pole from Scott Base. Now Fuchs had made it from Shackleton Base. Between them they had covered more than 2,000 miles across frozen Antarctica.

The cameras clicked for the last time and, as Dufek led Fuchs towards warmth and comfort, Fuchs looked at all of us, and said,

"We never expected so many people—this is hardly fair, you know!"

Inside the base, cables of congratulations were awaiting Fuchs, to signify his first major achievement—the covering of 930 desperately difficult miles since leaving his headquarters at Shackleton Base. It had taken much longer than was planned, but they were across the worst part of the continent. No wonder the London expedition headquarters cabled him "Warmest congratulations on reaching Pole. The endurance shown and progress already made over difficult and hitherto unexplored country strengthens still further the confidence we continue to have in you and your party."

Fuchs sent a cable to the Queen, reading: "Today the Commonwealth Trans-Antarctic Expedition reached the South Pole after travelling 930 miles from Shackleton Base. We are in good health and we look forward to departing in two days' time for the last stretch of our journey to Scott Base."

Soon a reply came from the Queen, "My husband and I send our warm congratulations to all members of the Commonwealth Trans-Antarctic party, and our best wishes for the next stage of your journey to Scott Base."

And to me, as we washed our hands in the Pole toilet, Fuchs said just this: "I'm on top of my form."

Once again, in close quarters, I found myself immensely impressed with the quiet efficiency of this man with pale blue eyes, ruddy complexion, and reddish blond beard, who behaved like the complete master of the expedition, not aggressive in any way, but quite definitely the boss. I remembered what Dufek had told me when we were discussing the two men, "Wait till you see Fuchs, Noel. He's a man in a million." The entire American station was enormously impressed with him and the intelligence and calmness with which he handled the questions of newspaper reporters, some of whom, as might be imagined, were anxious to discover the details of any rift between Fuchs and Hillary. He replied to every question quietly and in detail. He did not shirk any issue. He admitted being behind, but quietly emphasized, time and again, that if he did not reach Scott Base before winter, "Well, that's just too bad—it's a risk we must take."

There was so much to do it was hard to know where to begin. Lunch was overdue, but who could eat anything before looking through the great batch of mail from home, their first letters since November? One man received a picture of two beautiful girls across which was written, "You are always in our thoughts." But George Lowe, who was with Hillary on Everest, received the toughest letter. On top of his pile of mail was an envelope severely embossed "OHMS." It was his income tax demand. It had been sent to London, to Shackleton, taken by the expedition's Otter plane to Scott, flown by the Americans to the Pole. It certainly gave Lowe an added reason for trying to get out of Antarctica before winter set in, for March 7 was the last day for the income tax.

"We need a secretary for all this!" cried one man. But there was a note of sadness too. Among the letters was one for Dr. George Rogers, the physiologist, from his wife, telling him his father had died. But then to lunch—cheeseburgers. At the end of the lunch, Dr. Fuchs was presented with a large specially cooked "birthday cake," with the expedition's route traced in red icing sugar against a map of Antarctica.

So they were here. And now—what next? What were the perils ahead on the last great stage of the adventure, the Pole to Scott Base?

As far as terrain was concerned, Fuchs was now definitely "over the hump," but he had before him instead an even more diabolical enemy, the steadily worsening weather with its lowering temperatures. Fuchs was, by the time he reached the Pole, almost four weeks and 700 miles behind the schedule he had originally planned. It would, as I reported at the time, be quite wrong to suggest that in pushing on he faced any imminent danger. With the modern air rescue operations on hand, danger was not the most important factor; rather was it the need for determination and grit. It would have been quite possible for Fuchs to become snowbound for a long winter period, even, say, in the middle of the Skelton Glacier. In fact he could have stayed there an entire winter, a formidable test of endurance, but he would nevertheless be in no serious danger, since he could always be supplied by parachute.

Fuchs now faced a journey divided into two parts: From the Pole to Depot 700, alone; from Depot 700 down the Skelton, to Scott, accompanied by Hillary.

The first of these would, I reflected, be the easier—500 miles across the Polar plateau. It was true that Hillary had found some going very slow because of deep snow, but this would not affect Fuchs so much because the Sno-Cats were much more suitable for soft snow than Hillary's Fergusons. Depot 700 could well be the critical point of the whole trip—more critical than the Pole. If Fuchs could make 700 in good time, all well and good. But if he were subjected to more harassing delays like those on the way to the Pole, he might arrive at 700 too late to be guaranteed air support. The Skelton Glacier was a very tough problem, even with Hillary to lead the Sno-Cats down a marked trail that Hillary knew by heart. For now the weather would play an increasingly vital part in the fortunes of the expedition. The general belief at the Pole (later happily to be confounded) was that Fuchs could almost certainly not reach Scott Base before the Antarctic winter set in early in March. This anxiety was shared privately by some of the expedition members. When one of them said how good it would be to spend two days at the Pole, I remarked that with the heavy program of vehicle maintenance, he would probably have to stay three. He looked thoroughly alarmed and said, "But God! We can't afford even one more day if we're to get out in time!"

Hillary was, of course, still prepared to fly out and meet Fuchs at 700. He said so to me again the day before Fuchs arrived at the Pole, but he also repeated his previous warnings that it was very difficult to fly anybody out from the altitude of 700 so late in the season. In deciding to go on from the Pole, Fuchs had to face the slight possibility that the weather could be so bad Hillary would be unable to fly out to meet him at Depot 700, simply because a plane could not land, or even if it could land, could not take off again. Fuchs would then have to make up his mind whether or not to try and descend the Skelton Glacier without Hillary's help.

By now every day was indeed counting, as the expedition member had said. It was a race between Fuchs and the weather.

"And what do you think of the chances?" I asked Fuchs that afternoon.

"I see no reason why we shouldn't, with reasonable luck, reach Scott Base by the first week in March. We are leaving the dogs at the Pole (they were later flown out by the Americans) and that will mean we shall no longer be limited to the maximum of 30 miles a day which is the limit dogs can travel each day."

He emphasised that the expedition "would certainly continue the work in accordance with our scientific program."

"We came here," he added, "with the idea of doing scientific work—the aspect of adventure is only secondary. It would be quite fruitless merely going from A to B and doing nothing but make the journey."

"The route from here to Scott Base should be much easier," explained Fuchs, "now that we have depots and Hillary's assistance. We plan to drop one Weasel on the way if necessary. We have already abandoned three vehicles. People have suggested it would be easier to split our trip, but I ask those who make that suggestion if they are prepared to pay for it. Hillary's suggestion that we stop at the Pole was merely a suggestion—not an argument—and I didn't accept it. As far as Hillary's dash to the Pole is concerned, it did not interfere with us, so good luck to him. I have not yet had the chance of a good talk with Ed."

What about the arrangements for the next section of the trip?

"Well, I am quite satisfied that we can get to Depot 700 without any extra fuel."

There was the little matter of Depot 800, which Hillary might have formed for Fuchs.

"Yes, we would perhaps have liked an extra depot at 800, but I am quite satisfied with what has been done."

Hillary sat next to Fuchs at lunch, and immediately afterwards, Fuchs returned to his "office." The two men did not have a serious talk together for at least five hours after Fuchs' arrival. There was something very pathetic about the whole business. Only a short time ago at the Pole I had witnessed the excitement of Hillary's arrival, the moment when that great lumbering giant with his tousled hair had grinned from his tractor and strode into the camp. The spotlight of the world's attention had fallen on him as Fuchs fought his way towards South Ice. Now it was all changed. Fuchs was the man of the moment, not only for his achievement, but because already the world was divided in its opinion of Hillary's dash. While Fuchs quietly took himself off to work or read letters or sleep, poor Hillary, yesterday's hero, mooched around the camp looking slightly forlorn and bewildered. It wasn't until after five o'clock—during which time Fuchs and Hillary had had no private conversation—that Hillary popped his tousled head round the door of my hut and asked plaintively: "Anybody seen Fuchs?"

While Fuchs and Hillary were having their little chat, I spent all the time possible with the expedition members, piecing together the days they had passed on the trail; what it was like for lonely men to push forward inch by inch, day by day, for almost two months across the world's most hostile land.

From Fuchs himself I had already heard of the events that led to the delay.

"Contributing factors," he said, "were that we originally planned to start on September 1 with a route-proving trip, but were late due to bad weather. We are now three weeks behind schedule. We can't blame ourselves for the delay, as we had to make a safe route. From now on we shall go quicker because we shall take seismic soundings at longer intervals—probably every forty miles instead of every thirty."

Geoffrey Pratt, the seismologist, said that a sounding only 25 miles from the Pole showed that the land—as apart from the ice covering—was 5,000 feet above sea level, compared with only 800 feet of solid land above sea level at the Pole. It was strange to think that beneath the utterly flat expanse of ice and snow on which we were standing, there were in fact violent peaks, deep valleys, lakes and submerged rivers in a continent hidden from man's eyes for countless centuries.

Geoffrey Pratt was a blond giant, almost 33 years old, unmarried, and sporting a fine golden beard. He shared a tent and tractor duties on the trail with a dark-bearded South African of 30, Hannes La Grange from Pretoria. Hannes helped Pratt with his seismic work and from these two men, I pieced together a sample day on the trail with Fuchs.

The day began at eight A.M. when Geoff (if it was his turn) got up and prepared breakfast of porridge, cocoa, biscuits, and some golden syrup, which was cooked on a small stove in the two-man tent and eaten in their sleeping bags—both men fully clothed, for neither undressed or washed once on the entire trip. Each slept in his tent on a ground sheet, then a blanket, and after that a sheepskin. The put their sleeping bags on top of all this. Hannes carried a pillow all the way and two sheets to put in his bag, but Geoff didn't bother with them. "I could never find my way into my sleeping bag with all that extra complication."

While Hannes started packing up some of the equipment and seeing to the Sno-Cat, Geoff usually prepared a cold snack for midday—biscuits, Marmite, cheese, some cold bacon, and biscuit sandwiches, together with three flasks of hot cocoa. The picnic lunch ready, Geoffrey had each morning to take his seismic shot while Hannes packed up the tent. By noon, the expedition was ready to leave.

Geoff and Hannes arranged their lives so that the man who was cook for the day also drove the tractor which pulled two sledges. They set off soon after noon, driving slowly forward when possible until eight P.M., a break in the middle about three o'clock for their cold lunch and hot cocoa. The five vehicles each stopped when they wished to. There was no general halt, and since they all stopped for a similar length of time, they would always catch each other up.

Each evening it took the two of them about ten minutes to put up their tent. Then they had an hour's work laying out seismic cables ready for the next morning. Then dinner which always—"but always!"—included the standby and the curse of Antarctica: pemmican. Each day they tried different ways to make this utterly tasteless food taste of something—adding everything from curry powder, dehydrated potatoes, to raisins and even cocoa! But no man has yet discovered a way of making pemmican taste pleasant.

"It tastes of nothing!" said Hannes.

"Rather horrible, whatever you do," said Geoff, adding, "And, unfortunately, pemmican has a smell which eventually comes out in a man himself if he keeps on eating it."

Dinner was never more than one course, with coffee or tea and the inevitable biscuits. This couple had a radio in their Sno-Cat, so they could, if they wished, even get the BBC from home. But, like all the others, they found that by the end of the day they were so fagged they hardly bothered listening in. The only time the news was really listened to was during the Fuchs-Hillary row— and what they heard on the radio was all they knew about it.

But it was difficult to talk too much to the boys, for most of them—though they would never have admitted it—were almost dropping with fatigue. I often wonder, now it is all over, whether they could really have made the second half of the journey without those unasked-for but accepted three days of warmth and good food and companionship at the Pole.

Griff Pugh, the physiologist who had been on Everest with Hillary, told me bluntly, "They are on the point of exhaustion." Pugh, who had been sent to Antarctica by the British Medical Research Council added:

"I shall tell Fuchs that his men require at least twenty-four hours in bed. Then they will be as fit as possible in this climate. But without such a rest, Fuchs is not going to get enough out of them when they take to the trail again."

The work of physiologists like Pugh, a blond giant with wavy hair and a passion for skiing, was of great importance, but it also had its amusing side. He took his work very seriously, his main job being to test scientifically the effects of the arduous trail life on the constitutions of the expedition members. One of the important ways to determine this exactly was to take samples of the urine from all the men, so that as the team approached, and the moment of Fuchs' glory appeared at hand, we were treated to the spectacle of Griff Pugh darting around with plastic bottles, each carefully labelled with a man's name, and with a space for the exact time when the sample would be made available.

Because the first drink and first meal would radically change the basic constitution of the men, Griff darted around begging the men not to go to the toilet without their little bottles, and then begging them not to touch a drop of food or drink until the bottles had been used. Since he also had to take temperatures and blood tests before any food or drink was absorbed into the body, the slightly bewildered Fuchs team had a pretty rough time of it— when all they were thinking about, with slavering lips, was their first good meal for two months or more. The Pole dining room, with its line of bottles and phials of blood, looked like a dispensary until Chet Segers, the cook, asked rather plaintively, "Can I please start to set the table!"

The Pole was so crowded during the stay of Fuchs and the Admiral's party that we had to eat our meals in two sittings. Really, quite a busy little place! From my first visit, when I had been the only reporter at the Pole, the press corps had now grown to six, including a *Times* photographer, Stuart Heydinger, who had even brought his own portable photo-radio transmitting machine, in the hope that he would be the first man in the world to transmit a radio photo directly from the Pole. It was an ingenious machine which plugged into any suitable radio transmitting station, and when I asked him why he had come so far so late, and why—in view of *The Times*'s interest in the Fuchs expedition—he had not reached Antarctica earlier, in time to greet Hillary at the Pole, he answered, with his tongue in his cheek: "Old boy, *The Times* didn't know anybody could get to the Pole. They only decided to send me when they read you were here!"

Heydinger had bad luck, and failed in his dream. He took magnificent photographs of Fuchs' arrival—far and away the best taken—and what is more, he also brought his own portable developing kit, and had them ready to transmit in a few minutes. But somehow he could not get a radio link out of the Pole, even though we were able to get cables out. It was bad luck.

We did not have much time at the Pole with Fuchs; the small base was so crowded we had to get out quickly in order to give our beds to the expedition members. And quite right, too. But again I must say how impressed I was with Fuchs, who fitted in perfectly into the camp. With his innate good manners and charm, he was liked instantly. Vernon and Mogy made no secret of their admiration for the man; and of course by now the details of the row had reached the Pole, and the opinion of the Pole base members was all in favor of Fuchs. And they noticed, as everybody did, the way Hillary and Fuchs appeared ill at ease in each other's company; or at least, in the rare occasions when they were together, not ebullient in their friendship.

As for myself, I was too busy to be concerned, even though I noticed. I wanted to use these last hours at the Pole to bring into sharp focus some of the results of the scientific work, and the way in which Fuchs' work was being integrated with those of other scientists. In a book of this sort, written by a layman, one is always tempted to dwell on the adventurous aspect of such an expedition rather than the scientific achievements which, also, are sometimes difficult to translate into ordinary language.

But what Fuchs had done—and was doing—and what the other scientists had done—and were doing—was just as fascinating in its way as the story of life on the trail.

12. Scientific Work in Antarctica

Fuchs' scientific work formed but one part of the scientific explorations taking place across the entire continent and by scientists of ten nations. Fuchs' arrival at the Pole meant that he had already done work of an invaluable nature, in crossing from the Weddell Sea to the South Pole, over land never trodden before. As though he were a cartographer, he and Pratt had built up the first picture ever recorded of the "up and down" shape of Antarctica. But it was still only a section of the scientific jig-saw puzzle which the world's scientists were trying to piece together.

Perhaps the most colorful (but not necessarily the most important) discovery, shared by the Pole team, scientists at Little America, and doctors working with Fuchs, was that prehistoric man roaming Antarctica countless years ago probably had the same colds, headaches, and rheumatism as we do, for they found proof that bacteria existed in the dim past—bugs the same as we have in our bodies today, some for good, some for evil. This discovery confounded experts who had believed Antarctica to be bacteria-free. Indeed, we at McMurdo believed this to be so, and believed it to be the reason for our immunity to disease, from which we were virtually free in Antarctica the entire duration of my stay.

But then scientists on the trail and elsewhere began finding the first hints that there had been bacteria in Antarctica. The final proof came when a doctor found traces of bacteria in the South Pole snow-mine, which Fuchs went to inspect. With two sterilized picks, wrapped in polythene, the scientist descended ninety feet into the mine (which put the age of the ice at up to 3,000 years) and then dug out samples of the ice, placing them in sterilized containers. The ice contained bacteria. Immediately tests were made in other parts of Antarctica and the same results discovered.

It will take some time before the findings are analysed, but traces of bacteria were there, though present-day Antarctica is virtually bacteria-free. It is possible that bacteria existed many thousands of years ago, but disappeared—or were buried—when the ice closed in. This theory was advanced because of the difficulty of healing open wounds in Antarctica. At the Pole I cut my hand, not very seriously, but in two different places, so I underwent a "healing test." One wound was covered with plaster. It healed in six days; but the other was treated, yet still left open. It refused to heal until it was covered, due to my low skin temperature and the consequent reduced flow of blood in the fingers—but also due, it was thought, to the lack of bacteria that help in healing.

Griff Pugh, who was taking body tests on the Fuchs team, was also working with another physiologist, Major James Adams of the Royal Army Medical Corps, on human guinea pigs attached to Hillary's rear base at Scott. The doctors had devised fascinating devices for men to wear while working, in order to test the stresses on the human frame of men working in cold weather. These two doctors, Pugh, aged forty-seven, and Adams, just ten years younger, refused all efforts to live in the comfortable quarters of either Scott or McMurdo, but pitched their tent in the cold of the snow-bound pass that lined our two camps. It was a common sight to see Griff Pugh or Jim Adams out in the snow as I walked from one base to another. Naturally, on his visit to the Pole to see Fuchs or his team members, Pugh slept in a hut. He didn't want to, but aircraft space was so limited he could not carry tents as well as all his instruments and paraphernalia.

But in their own tent near Scott, each British doctor wore a suit of wire underclothes which was plugged into various instruments to determine the amount of energy they used. They—and any other men they could rope in—wore the suits for 24 hours at a stretch, the instruments being carried in specially-constructed pockets. By wearing the underclothes at night as well as during the day, they could measure the amount of energy a man stored up for the next day while sleeping in cold conditions, and their findings will eventually have decisive influence not only on the amount of energy required by any future cold weather explorers, but on our military machines, and such vital factors as the correct clothing for high-altitude flying or cold-weather land fighting. To make their findings more accurate, Pugh and Adams also experimented with the amounts of oxygen men used in cold-weather climates. Men chosen for the experiments wore special packs on their backs which measured oxygen consumption.

Though Hillary was unconcerned with scientific achievement, and blithely trotted towards the Pole with slight carbon monoxide poisoning, quite unaware of the stresses the cold weather was imposing on him, Dr. Fuchs and his team made the most careful scientific observations of the effects of cold on men. The expedition doctor was then able to present these to Griffith Pugh at the Pole so that, after he had taken his various tests, he could build up a picture of the cumulative effects of low temperatures, much more important than the effects of an isolated foray into cold weather.

Then Pugh was able to put Fuchs' carefully documented knowledge against experiments of another kind carried out at the Pole, where two men were sent out on the coldest day ever recorded in the world's history—minus 102 degrees—to see what would happen to them. With their faces covered by a parka that came right out in front of them, the two men managed to stay outside for three hours. Each one wore twenty-six pounds of clothes. The rubber thermo-boots of one man froze in the first five minutes. The canvas mukluks of the other did not freeze for over an hour. By the end of the experiment their body temperature had dropped one degree and each man had lost two pounds weight due to dehydration. After they had been undressed (their hands were too numb to do it themselves), both complained of dizziness and sickness but, even so, their experiment proved that properly clothed men can stand extreme cold for limited periods better than machines, and even better than the clothes they stand up in.

(I also, in a very minor manner, experimented on the difference between mukluks and thermo-boots, wearing each in turn on different days for half an hour at minus sixty. The thermo-boots, invented by the U.S. armed force, could be worn without socks, and kept my feet perfectly warm, but, because of the rubber casing, caused heavy sweating, most unpleasant in a country with such limited washing facilities. The mukluks, the same as worn by Scott, were much better with four pairs of socks. They kept my feet warm, and though the two outer pairs of socks were wet, the inner pairs were dry, and so were my feet.)

While men proved they could withstand extreme temperatures, all experience showed that the real limit for using machines effectively was minus fifty. After that the oil refused to flow and unknown stresses (as Fuchs was to discover just before Depot 700) affected metals in curious ways. I saw an astonishing thing happen at one camp, when the solid steel track frame of a bulldozer, fourteen feet long and weighing a ton, snapped like a piece of glass when bulldozing snow at minus forty-seven degrees. (At McMurdo there was another hazard to machines, for during the summer the volcanic dust mixed with slush and formed a natural grinding compound that quickly ruined all moving parts of engines.)

Aircraft, particularly, were subject to strains that grounded them when men could carry on at extremely low temperatures, one of the main problems being the droplets that formed through condensation in the air spaces of the petrol tanks. These would freeze and clog the fuel lines like a mass of tiny ball bearings.

As Fuchs made his way from South Ice, he also took the most careful weather observations, and here again his expedition played a part that no other men could play in building up the first complete picture of weather in Antarctica. The Americans, it is true, had dotted the continent with weather stations and most ingenious instruments called "grasshoppers," but their value was in giving current weather data, rather than studying weather conditions in order to find a general pattern.

The "grasshopper," as Dufek describes it, was "an interesting piece of equipment provided by the Naval Research Laboratory . . . that can be parachuted from an aircraft. When installed on an aircraft it resembles a bomb. Upon landing a device is automatically released which causes the legs of the apparatus to extend like a grasshopper's. Then it begins to chirp like a cricket while its antenna extends into the air. Soon, by its own mechanical efforts, it stands upright, ready for business. It then records its own readings of barometric pressure, wind direction, wind force, and temperature, and transmits this data automatically for distances up to 800 miles. The 'grasshopper' can operate for six weeks without servicing."

In its way the "grasshopper" was one of the most ingenious scientific instruments in Antarctica, and an invaluable guide for our aircraft, but the scientists wanted more data, for they were concerned about the possibility of flying commercial airlines across the South Pole when exact details had been discovered of the winds and temperatures in the upper air.

Fuchs, as I say, contributed greatly to this, working in an unexplored part of Antarctica while others released high altitude weather balloons from McMurdo, Little America, the Pole Station. Soon a strange and terrifying picture emerged of the air above us, moving in apparently predetermined patterns around hidden obstacles, for all the world like a stream burbling for centuries along the same path, around the same rocks, yet slowly, with the same centuries, changing course as its power wore away the obstacles in its path.

When the Polar weather research details are finally correlated, they will produce what is probably the first direct benefit to mankind of the scientific work which Fuchs and others were doing, and will without doubt eventually lead to the opening up of a South Pole air route as safe as that on which I have flown comfortably near the North Pole. Already we had discovered the pattern of polar night jet streams, high above the world's most forbidding terrain. These air streams travel in gently curving paths 50,000 feet above the frozen continent. Between June and October, in the dead of the Antarctic night, they move from west to east. One day, without doubt, air lines using those winds at the proper times will be able to leapfrog over the Antarctic from South America or South Africa to Australia or New Zealand.

The temperature changes of long summers and winters—the long days and nights—were, the scientists discovered, making these air masses rotate close to each other rather like the rollers of a wringing machine, with the jet stream coming out like a shirt put through the wringer, at a speed of 150 miles an hour or more.

But equally important, though hard to believe, the weather at the South Pole has a direct bearing on the weather as far away as London or New York or Paris; and therefore, without any doubt, accurate knowledge of weather data at the Pole can help the rest of the world to know more of their local weather conditions. This was a major reason for keeping on the Pole station after the IGY had ended. The U.S. Navy's brilliant meteorologist, Commander John Mirabeto (with whom I was to fly out of Antarctica) summed it up to me:

"The Pole station is vital to us in making accurate and informed weather assessments because much of the world's weather hinges on what happens on the Polar plateau and in Antarctica. If we don't know what is going on at the Pole, then we cannot know what is going on in Antarctica with certainty. And if we don't know what is going on in Antarctica, then we cannot forecast what the weather is going to be like with any degree of certainty in Britain or America."

Far-fetched? Not at all. Antarctica is the world's largest natural refrigerator, containing eighty-four per cent of the world's ice, and naturally, as one scientist explained it to me, "it is the world's most efficient cold air factory." For the first time, with Fuchs helping, scientists were proving that the weather at the South Pole has a far greater effect on the weather of the rest of the world than mankind believe. The Pole, central pivot of an enormous land mass buried under shifting ice, is inevitably the hub of atmospheric circulation in the southern hemisphere, and the winds and blizzards which we encountered did not just vanish into thin air. As John Mirabeto said, they affected the weather the whole world over.

But all this weather data had to be collated, including the weather reports from Fuchs. This was an immense task. All weather information in Antarctica was relayed to a depot called Weather Central, situated at Little America, another U.S. Navy station built at the other end of the Ross Ice Shelf, about 400 miles from Mc-Murdo and about 800 miles from the Pole. Here scientists, living in snow-covered huts with leaking tunnels joining them, and on ice that was moving daily five feet nearer to the open sea, prepared daily weather maps covering the entire Antarctic continent, available not only to pilots flying to the Pole, but as a permanent record of weather trends.

Thus, if only to study the weather of the world, the Pole station had to be kept running, even after the conclusion of the geophysical year. And in this connection, Fuchs and Hillary between them may have laid the foundations for a great practical plan to keep the Pole going—a highway from the Ross Sea to the Pole itself, a possible land route for future use by American scientists to obviate both the immense cost and the ever-present danger of keeping the station supplied by air. Hillary had said when I first met him at the Pole that he thought it perfectly feasible to have a highway to the Pole, and now Fuchs confirmed it.

"It is entirely possible," he agreed. "The Americans have the equipment here, the men, the know-how. The ability of tractor machinery to operate in extreme temperatures and the altitudes of the

Polar plateau has been proved by Sir Edmund Hillary's march to the South Pole, using tractors designed for nothing more complicated than towing ploughs or pulling carts in farmyards."

This is no dream, but what Fuchs was too modest to mention was that without his and Hillary's land journeys, the Americans would be working in an unknown wilderness. Now, despite the seasonal changes that would make new crevasses, the Commonwealth team would in fact have charted and mapped a complete route, for one of the most amazing engineering projects ever envisaged—a highway the 1,250 miles from McMurdo to the Pole. What is more, I am convinced that, solely as a result of the Fuchs expedition, the Americans will make that road, for the simple reason (overlooked by those who sneer at the "milk run" Polar flights) that the danger factor will be considerably less on land than in the air.

Trigger Hawkes, whom I had met first in Christchurch, and to whom all flying was "no strain," knew about those hazards— and about the cost. It is hard to realise it, but one Globemaster crashing on the Polar run would cost the Americans supplying the Pole twice as much as the entire Trans-Antarctic Expedition which may one day result in a Polar highway.

"After all," said Trigger Hawkes, "you can take a pitcher to the well too often. If you fly too often in Antarctica you are bound to go down or get into bad trouble sometime. The Globemaster, our ninety-ton parachute-supply and troop-carrying plane, costs nearly 3 million dollars. We've lost one already. Twenty engines on these planes have given out.

"Next we use the Neptune patrol bombers with two reciprocating and two jet engines to assist take-off at the Pole. Each plane costs about 2 million dollars. Each Jato rocket bottle costs $400 and we use sixteen each time we take off at the Pole, to get the plane up in the rarefied air. We have already lost one Neptune and the four men who flew in it.

"The Dakota with its special equipment (the Old Charger) costs around 1 million dollars. Each time a pilot takes off he does so knowing that he may not have an airfield to land on when he gets back owing to fog or the ice runway giving out. Furthermore, scientific gear is often smashed on impact during parachute drops at the Pole. So, since there is a vital necessity to keep the South Pole station open, there is also a vital necessity to open a trail to take all or some of the load off the aviators."

If this dream ever becomes reality, it will be almost entirely due to Fuchs and Hillary.

And what of the land beneath the air and atmosphere which was of such importance to scientists? Here the seismic findings of Fuchs were helping to build up a picture of the shape of the continent, covered in parts by ice 8,000 feet thick. Though it may not melt for millennia to come, what lies underneath is a matter of important scientific interest. (Incidentally, if the ice of Antarctica did melt, it would increase the height of the sea level at every waterside in the world by 200 feet, flooding the world's coastal areas.)

Fuchs was helping to find out what lay beneath this shroud of ice. Antarctica, the land of Antarctica, had usually been regarded as the highest continent of the world, up to two miles above sea level at its highest point. But now we know that the Pole rests on land only a few hundred feet above sea level, thanks to the first seismic soundings taken by Father Linehan, the Jesuit seismologist of Boston College. Another scientist discovered that Byrd Station, which man believed to be 5,000 feet above sea level, was resting on 10,000 feet of ice, so that actually Byrd was built over a hollow 5,000 feet below sea level—i.e., a frozen lake. Fuchs, almost within sight of the Pole itself, found solid ground 5,000 feet above sea level —in effect a great mountain towering below the small hill of the Pole, if one could strip away the ice.

Dr. Fuchs' seismic work in a part of Antarctica hitherto never trodden by man fitted in perfectly with the studies in glaciology and geology that were being undertaken by the other nations involved. Not only would it permit man to draw up a map of the hidden continent, but would help the glaciologists who were trying to determine one basic unanswered question: whether the ice on the Polar Cap is receding or growing. This they were doing by taking samples at different depths which determined the age of the ice—which were then sent regularly to the United States to be examined for radioactive forces of oxygen and hydrogen.

Fuchs was also finding out, in the greatest detail possible, how men could live in the world's toughest climate, a climate without vegetation, without life, and in the higher altitudes with a short supply of oxygen. It is one step farther to find out how men can live in space when, in the very near future, that problem arises.

Dr. Rogers, of the Fuchs expedition, was investigating some fascinating problems. Why was it possible that after three months in the cold, a man could pick up a can of nearly boiling water without burning his fingers? I saw Fuchs himself lay his hand on a kettle on the hob without apparently feeling it at all. And what gasses were there in the breath of a man living at subzero temperatures? Dr. Rogers had even managed to send back tins full of breath to be analysed. At the same time, Rogers was regularly pinching the skin of his colleagues on the trail with special forceps to measure their fat layer thickness. At times they had to work with special masks on their faces. He took regular coloured photographs of their fingers and toes.

It was not difficult to see the force of Dr. Fuchs' character after I had met him at the Pole; nor was it difficult to see why he was apparently so unconcerned about the possibility of spending another winter in Antarctica, a prospect which dismayed Hillary. Fuchs' complete disregard of the passage of any time began to take on a new perspective when one talked quietly to him about the scientific achievement of his expedition.

By the time Fuchs reached the Pole and was taking his first shower, much had been discovered. He had already revolutionized world knowledge of the mineral wealth of Antarctica by chipping a lump of pure anthracite out of an Antarctic mountain, which proved that this ice desert was once tropical jungle. And where there is coal from living matter, there could be oil.

Long before the terrible journey captured the world's headlines, the expedition had spent a winter in Antarctica not loafing around in their huts, but pursuing science, when the expedition dug a hole fifty feet into the ice. All the way down the hole they noted each season's layer of snow back over the years, and so made a polar weather chart reaching back into history. Along the entire trek towards the Pole (and to be continued) members of the expedition had taken it in turns to get up every three hours during the night and walk through the night to read their weather instruments.

As *The Times* rightly said, in a leading article on January 4, "The time Dr. Fuchs takes is not of primary importance; his object is not the destination but the journey itself; for he is on a voyage of discovery, and it is by the extent of the scientific information he gathers on the way that the value of the whole expedition . . . is to be judged. They are all in the Antarctic with the same hope of adding to the sum of human knowledge as the researchers of many nationalities working for the International Geophysical Year.

"It is far too early to estimate what may come of the new knowledge he and the other explorers will bring home," added *The Times*. "But many will remember the bold imaginations of Sir Raymond Priestley at the British Association in 1956, when he suggested that some day the Antarctic might be a storehouse for the world's surplus food against a day of famine for an ever-increasing population; that atomic-powered settlements might be planted on the mainland; that the Antarctic gales might be harnessed as another source of power; and that man may yet find a way to overcome the latent heat of ice and add a seventh continent to the six he already has in thrall."

At the moment when Fuchs was preparing for the second great stage of his journey, Science's assault on the Antarctic was reaching the middle point of the IGY. The work had gone on for nearly nine months out of the eighteen of the "year" and Fuchs was only one of more than forty scientific bases in Antarctica. The fact that his was a movable base made his work all the more important.

13. *On to Scott Base*

Towards the evening of the day when Fuchs arrived at the Pole, the time came for me to leave. I half-expected Hillary to stay after all and escort Bunny Fuchs across the plateau, but no, he decided to return with us. A Neptune bomber was flown up for us and landed on the strip around tea time.

We loaded our gear while Jack Coley had a cup of coffee and a sandwich and then all moved out to the strip to clamber aboard. There was the usual period of waiting—rather like saying good-by to friends at a railway station—and once again I noticed that Fuchs, who had walked out to say farewell, kept himself apart from Hillary. It was not that the two refused to speak to each other—Fuchs' manners were far too immaculate for any nonsense like that—but Hillary stood several yards away talking to one group, while Fuchs talked to another.

This, I felt sure, would be the last time I ever saw the South Pole—but it was a near thing getting off, and an expensive one. We all managed to squeeze aboard the Neptune jammed tightly on the floor, with Jack Coley at the controls. In the bitter cold we had all said our farewells. The ground crew loaded up the outside of the belly with sixteen Jato bottles in the racks. Jack Coley maneuvred the Neptune, with its scarlet wing tips, to the edge of the runway, and then let her go. With the weight and altitude, the old plane lumbered along slowly down the runway, gathering very little speed. Then Coley pressed the button that fired the Jato bottles—sixteen of them at $400 each—and a terrific roar shook the plane. She gathered speed, but still not enough. Cooped up on the floor I could not see a thing. I was next to the navigator, an old friend from previous flights who could tell how the Jatos were behaving. He crossed his fingers. Then the speed seemed to slacken, and there was an unpleasant jerk. We had run into soft snow at the end of the runway. Down went the thumbs of the navigator.

"No go!" he shouted above the engine noise. "Some of the bottles didn't fire," then added from the bottom of his heart, "what a mucking way to earn a living."

Fuchs and Mogy and Vern were still at the edge of the airstrip. We taxied back and clambered out. Due to a bad electrical circuit, four Jato bottles had not fired. The other twelve had, so bang went $4,800. But even with twelve Jato bottles, we did not have enough "push" to get off from the deck.

On the edge of the airstrip, we all decided what to do next. To Coley's horror, he discovered that the entire Jato stock at the Pole consisted of eight more bottles. Four were left on the aircraft (the four that hadn't fired) so that made twelve—the same number that had proved insufficient to get us airborne. So, naturally, it was decided to send only half the passengers, and obviously Hillary and Dufek and Merle Macbain had pride of place. Off they went—the first time I had seen from the ground the magnificent visual effects of Jato bottles being fired against the white snow.

As we stood (wondering when we should ever get off), Coley fired the twelve bottles half way down the runway. The whole outside of the plane's belly was covered with vivid flames. Then the thrust of the bottles tore at the snow below. As we watched, the hot blast vaporised the snow surface of the runway and the cold air immediately condensed the vapour to leave a fog curtain, white and purple and red, half a mile long behind the aircraft, which was like a tiny insect, far into the white desert, with an enormous train, like a wedding train, streaming behind.

But again the Neptune couldn't take off. Even with the reduced load the twelve bottles were not enough at that altitude. Bang went another $4,800! Again the Neptune turned round, but now she was stuck in deep snow, having overshot the runway again, and she had the devil of a job to get back on to the runway.

This was becoming slightly ridiculous, with all of us, including Fuchs and several members of his team, standing on the edge of the ice runway. But this time there was nothing to be done. No Jato left. We all tramped back to the Pole, to see the friends to whom we had said good-by. There we called up McMurdo on the radio, and did the only thing possible—arranged for another aircraft to fly up with a stock of Jatos sufficient for both planes to take off. That meant a wait of at least seven hours, including the time to prepare the aircraft at McMurdo and assemble the crew. Nothing to do but take off all our cold weather clothing, dive for the coffee pots, and wait for Chet Segers to cook us some dinner.

Though this sort of thing was "strictly routine" (to use the Navy's favourite phrase in Antarctica), I could not help reflecting that it did not augur well for the air support that Fuchs was expecting later on as he approached Depot 700. If an aircraft could be stranded because four out of sixteen Jato bottles did not fire, how could the Otter or Beaver from Scott Base—pitifully underpowered in comparison with the Neptunes—ever hope to take off in temperatures that would most certainly be much lower?

"We'll be at 700 in a couple of weeks," said Fuchs confidently, but I wondered.

We finally took off at two in the morning, in two planes, each using sixteen Jatos, splitting the passenger load so that the take-off alone had cost $12,800! But even this was not the end of our troubles. The first Neptune landed at McMurdo around breakfast time, half an hour before the one in which I was passenger. So wicked is the Antarctic weather that when the first Neptune landed the weather was perfect, cloudless. Yet by the time we were over-head, the airstrip was blotted out, completely hidden by a thick cloud which lay below us like a neat round blob of cotton wool. Half a mile from the strip, the camp itself with its orange huts, was perfectly visible. Two miles the other way, we could see Scott Base. But Scott Base's airstrip was not long enough for the Neptune to land on. It was a most eerie sensation. The cloud covered up the airstrip, but nothing else. All around was blazing in brilliant sun-shine. We made half a dozen runs to try and pierce the cloud, but it was no good. There was not a hope of landing.

There was nothing to do but, after radio consultation with base, land on the raw ice of the Sound. Eight miles away, the ice-breaker *Glacier* was resting in a channel she had cut a mile or so in from the open sea. It was decided to land near to her, as the ship itself would give us an important indication of height, and the chan-nel of almost black water would also act as a guide.

But firstly, we had to get rid of some excess petrol, for the danger of landing on raw ice is that one cannot see clearly the depth of any *sastrugi* or ice build ups. It was better to be on the safe side. We droned over the Ross Sea for two hours using up petrol, catching occasional glimpses of the world outside from the window in the rear of the cabin. As we did this, McMurdo sent out a stream of Weasels to line up, each one fifty yards distance from the next, so as to mark a rough airstrip for landing. I caught a glimpse of the fire engines crawling along the ice. The channel of water from the *Glacier* marked the other side of the strip. In actual fact we made a perfect landing. No strain at all, to use Trigger Hawkes's favourite expression. But I am the first to admit I did not have much appe-tite for breakfast.

Now there was nothing to do but settle down in McMurdo and wait for the good doctor—and keep an anxious eye on the calendar. The Pole was behind me. We had to make the best job of a boring time with almost no work to do, for Fuchs was now in direct contact with Scott Base, where *The Times* representative had swift facilities for cabling to New Zealand. There was little we could do to compete with him, as our radio from McMurdo to New York worked only twice a day, and if news reached us via Scott Base we might have to wait five or six hours before getting it out of McMurdo, whereas *The Times* man could whip it out as quickly as he liked.

We arranged to make a nightly telephone call to Hillary at Scott Base to be informed of the latest progress, which meant in effect that there was really nothing for anybody to do until a quarter-past five each evening.

I read a great deal, mostly during the night, and tried as best I could to sleep during the mornings. Even the movie had lost its thrill. Nobody played a game of bridge, nobody was looking for a game of poker. It was very dull and people's tempers began to shorten as we waited for news.

The whole of this time was the most trying of my three months in Antarctica, but though at times the close proximity in which we all lived and the lack of any privacy caused minor quarrels, on the whole the men in Antarctica managed to get on well together. There were surly members of the fraternity, but one learned to leave them alone; and the attitude of the officers to myself and other correspondents was so overwhelmingly cooperative as to be almost embarrassing. They couldn't have been more helpful. Not only this, the very rigours of Antarctica bound men together far more solidly than if they had been at some naval station back home in the United States. In my diary dated December 29, I wrote:

"One can understand that there is no time here for hate among the men whom destiny has planted in such unfertile soil. And I must say I have found in Antarctica a comradeship I had forgotten existed. It did exist when I was in the war, but war brought its train of beastliness as well. When I needed warmer gloves the other day, somebody cheerfully got out of bed at four in the morning to rummage around and find them for me. On my first journey to the Pole, I discovered that my thermo-boots were too warm for every-day camp wear. I immediately found myself with the offer of several pairs—in a climate where the loss of a boot means the loss of a life.

"Here all must join in the fight for survival and though life in Antarctica goes on with a grin, danger and loneliness are the constant companions of the men who live here. An aircraft nosedives on the softening ice of the runway; a helicopter in a whiteout flies blindly into ice no pilot can see. A few days ago I saw the priest who survived, though badly burned, in this helicopter crash. He gave a short and painfully wonderful sermon lying on his stretcher. A Weasel goes out across the ice and suddenly the ice cracks and five men inside are plunged into the water. That happened recently too. Four of the men were unable to get out of the death trap."

At times we were on the verge of quarrels, but they rarely seemed to mature, perhaps because people were afraid of quarrelling. One of McMurdo's chaplains, Father John Condit, who had wintered over, used to say life was too tough to quarrel.

"A year down here has made the younger men older and the older men younger," he said. "Hard life puts ten years of maturity into the boys. And it subtracts ten from the cynical older men who believed they had life all figured out. Human values, they discovered, were really the essence of everything. Down here you have to find something good in a man or it becomes unbearable. You just can't live with someone this closely and keep on hating him. It takes too much energy."

Back on the trail, Fuchs was plodding along to Depot 700, but he was going to be in trouble again before he reached it.

With the help of the Pole team, his engineers had overhauled the Sno-Cats for the journey across the plateau in weather that would get colder every day. How long would it take to reach 700? Hillary's last words as we left the Pole were, "Well, hope to see you in a fortnight, Bunny!" And Fuchs did not expect to take any longer either. The going promised to be good, the machines were in excellent condition, and they were more suitable for soft snow than Hillary's Fergusons had been.

But there were a lot of unknown factors, not only the problem of flying in cold weather, but the effects of the cold on the machines in which Fuchs was travelling. Illness. Breakdowns. Crevasses. A thousand things could happen. Some of them did. And very soon too.

The start of his trek across the plateau confounded all the pessimists. Despite uncompromising weather, biting winds, temperatures of nearly 20 below, partial whiteouts, and heavy drifting snow, Fuchs made 80 miles in the first two days, taking seismic soundings each evening. It was a wonderful start, in the race against the winter. For the winter was drawing on. As Fuchs camped for the second night on the plateau, two Neptunes made the last flight to the Pole for seven months—to bring out the dogs that Fuchs had used until he reached the Pole. They either had to be flown out by the Americans, or butchered. Fuchs offered to have them killed, but Dufek, despite worsening conditions, flew them out to Scott Base for Fuchs.

When the two Neptunes returned to McMurdo, and Fuchs was starting his third day's trek, Jack Coley found preparations ready for an immediate evacuation, if necessary, of all aircraft from McMurdo. Enormous crevasses were appearing on the ice in front of the camp. The blue-black sea, which had once been eight or nine miles away, was now only five miles from the camp. The strips were in danger of cracking up at a moment's notice. The planes on the strip were being kept fully fuelled, their crews at action stations, ready to take off at twenty minutes' notice.

At Scott, Hillary was making his preliminary plans for setting off to Depot 700 to meet Fuchs and lead him in, always presuming he could fly. Certainly this story could not be said to lack dramatic interest. Day after day, since I first flew in, crisis upon crisis had kept it moving to its climax. When I first reached the Pole, and cabled my dispatches, the expedition was in the doldrums. Thinking after my first week's cables that the people of Britain had had enough of a diet of snow and ice, I was reducing my work when —bang—Hillary set off for the Pole. That over, the quarrel between Fuchs and Hillary hit the headlines; the matter was settled, on the surface anyway. Then Fuchs reached the Pole. Now it looked like a fortnight of doldrums again. But not at all. At the very moment

when we in McMurdo were settling down to a period of dull waiting, there was high drama again.

Firstly, as the world discussed the dangers of flying in the
approaching winter, my old friend Gus Shinn ran into trouble on
the plateau, as though to give public warning of the threatened
dangers. Flying the Old Charger from the U.S. Naval station of
Little America, he was forced down on the Polar plateau when his
port engine started a serious oil leak. In order to repair the engine
before all his oil had gone, Gus—who was at that moment on the
plateau 334 miles from the Pole—decided to land. As he did so,
his ski undercarriage (always a weak point in the planes because
they were essentially makeshift affairs) smashed. It was impossible
to take off, even had he repaired the port engine. Gus and his crew
of four, the same men who had flown me to the Pole the first time,
were stranded on the plateau.

I was to see an impressive demonstration of the way the Americans could move into high gear in times of emergency, as they would
indeed have to if Fuchs were in trouble.

In case of fire, Shinn and his crew left their aircraft and, with
the survival gear and tents carried on every Antarctic flight, established a camp near the plane, in one of the loneliest parts of the continent. They had survival rations of pemmican for thirty days. They
were at an altitude of 4,000 feet. They spent the night there, and
the next day a relief DC3 flew out from Little America with a
spare undercarriage and the tools necessary to repair the oil leak.
No harm came of this mishap, but again it served to warn the world
of the dangers of flying.

They were even more impressively demonstrated within the
next few days, for suddenly, just as Fuchs seemed to be doing so
well, Geoff Pratt, the seismologist who had told me so much about
his life on the trail, was taken seriously ill. Fuchs was well on the way
towards Depot 700—150 miles from the Pole—when what might
have been a fatal disaster struck the expedition—and again forced
them to call upon the Americans for help, this time to save a life.

Pratt got carbon monoxide poisoning, apparently from cooking in his tent. This is a highly dangerous illness with grave lasting effects if not cured very quickly, and the only cure is to wash out the poison with abundant supplies of oxygen, one of the components of fresh air in short supply at the altitude of the Polar plateau.

The news first reached McMurdo at 4:25 on the afternoon of January 28 when Fuchs, after frantically trying to call Scott Base on his radio, finally called up McMurdo. He had made no contact with Scott despite repeated efforts, probably due to the fact that Scott, a small base, only kept radio watches at certain times of the day and night. The Americans, though, kept a twenty-four hour a day watch on an Antarctica emergency wave length. Fuchs was forced to use it.

Dufek acted quickly. As he got a message through to Hillary (the phone between McMurdo and Scott was down), aircrews for two Neptunes were assembled. Fuchs asked the Americans bluntly if it were possible to fly up oxygen to Pratt, who was by now lying on a stretcher in a Sno-Cat after twice collapsing. He was in serious trouble, and, incredible though it may seem in an expedition so well equipped, Fuchs had with him on the trail only 200 liters of oxygen, not nearly enough to cure Pratt. Within ten minutes of receiving the news, the first of two Neptunes (already fuelled for an emergency take-off) was ready for the flight to the Polar Cap. Jack Coley was to pilot it. Another Neptune would fly up as an emergency plane in case one was forced down. It had been expected at first that Coley would land the Neptune close to Fuchs, but the weather made this impossible. As Dufek said: "If the man were dying, we would land as many planes as Dr. Fuchs required, but our doctor here says it's the oxygen he needs, not a doctor, so in view of the bad flying conditions, we'll parachute it down."

Coley carried with him two oxygen cylinders each containing 6,000 liters of oxygen, and an automatic oxygen inhaling mask for Dr. Rogers, who was with Fuchs on the trail.

As the airstrip at McMurdo suddenly became alive with maintenance crews preparing the Neptunes, Scott Base moved into action. Hillary and Griffith Pugh came across the two miles in a Ferguson tractor ready to fly up to Fuchs if it was decided to land the Neptune. The McMurdo doctor meanwhile held a voice conference on the radio with the doctor on the plateau to determine the extent of the illness.

Pratt apparently had collapsed the previous day, but had managed, with the aid of his tent mate, to keep it secret. On this day he collapsed again and was, according to the doctor, "jerking convulsively," which indicated how advanced was the poisoning. But, even so, the doctors decided, in view of the bad weather, that it was not necessary to risk a landing. Jack Coley flew up, the oxygen was parachuted safely and, thanks entirely to the U.S. Navy, Pratt fully recovered in a few days.

Time was running short, so Fuchs tucked Pratt down on a stretcher in a Sno-Cat, and the lonely tractor moved on—towards Depot 700 and the last run home.

14.   The End of the Journey

THE epic crossing was drawing to its end. Fuchs was all but on the outskirts of Depot 700 and Hillary was waiting, ready to fly up. And then, just as Fuchs was about to get into trouble in the crevassed area south of 700, we in McMurdo and Scott had troubles of our own.

For some weeks the open sea had slowly been edging in and the American aircraft had been in a state of readiness to take off instantly—before sinking. But the speed with which the ice was melting had not for some time been apparent. One noticed there was more sea. The ice was forbidden except on business. A couple of Weasels went almost under and were regained with difficulty, not more than two miles from McMurdo. Coming back from a flight in an Otter, my Weasel broke through the ice, and we had to jump for it. Thin layers of ice formed bridges similar in their own way to the bridges over crevasses. It was very dangerous.

But then, with the weather still unseasonably warm, the small cracks extended into large ones. Soon enormous floes started calving. One day—two days before Fuchs arrived at Depot 700—the sea, which had not so long before been five miles away, came round as far as Hut Point, not a mile from the camp. That night the sea broke in still farther and the ten-foot ice that made McMurdo Sound as solid as dry land seemed to be breaking up, as it had done nearly fifty years ago when Scott was at Hut Point and had had to take a rowing boat to get round the point.

When we woke in the morning, Commander Ed Ludemans, the Admiral's commander of McMurdo, and I went to look at the truly appalling sight.

"I feel an old man this morning," groaned Ed. "We lost a hundred square miles of ice last night."

So we had. The entire icefield in front of the small hill on which McMurdo was built was covered with yawning holes. Even the small ski runway for the "inside Antarctica" flights had an enormous crevasse within fifty yards of the runway and running its entire length. The Neptunes made ready to take off, and left as soon as possible. Gus Shinn installed portable extra rubber tanks, and then set off in the Old Charger to make the trip to New Zealand. Only the light Otter and the helicopter could remain, because they could be hauled on to dry land.

If the water were to come in any closer, it would completely change the picture. Even now, or within the few hours necessary to fly out the last plane, Bunny Fuchs would be—as far as the Americans were concerned—on his own. There was still hope of a sudden drop in temperature which would make safe the new runway built for Globemasters three miles out into the Sound where the ice was thickest. But it was a fantastic spectacle. The natural question everybody asked was: "Well, if the planes can't land here, you could send in an icebreaker, I suppose?" But the answer to that was that it would take ten days for a breaker to arrive, and during that time the picture could change again, and with heavy freezing endanger the ship. Then it would be too cold for planes, which Dufek had forbidden to fly at temperatures below minus fifty.

Out on the ice, empty tractors and sledges with their scarlet or orange colours dotted the white and blue ice, in danger of sinking as huge chunks of ice broke away. The water was coming in like a slow, relentless tidal wave, an enormous gash of dark blue-black right in front of the camp, shaped like a great arrow head—and with roughly the same effect.

This was the picture at base as Fuchs trundled along toward Depot 700. His run from the Pole across the plateau had been remarkable. In three marches his party covered one hundred miles, travelling twenty-five, thirty-five, and forty miles on successive days. Seismic soundings had been taken, and he continued this remarkable speed till he was nearly within sight of Depot 700—almost as though he knew of the threatening dangers back at Scott Base and the very serious possibility of having to winter over.

For those of us now waiting at McMurdo, this was also a very personal problem, but with his characteristic swift action Admiral Dufek put at rest the minds of the correspondents, by promising them that if air transport were unavailable, he would keep the American icebreaker in waters as close as possible to Ross Island until March 10. This immediately meant that the small vessel *Endeavour*, used for the expedition, would also be able to stay, with the guarantee of a breaker to carve out a channel for her if the ice got too tough. For the first time, we began to feel that Fuchs might have a chance to get out before the winter.

Then, just before Depot 700, Fuchs lost the trail and fell into serious crevasse trouble. He was only a few miles from the cairns of 700, and one could not help reflecting how much time would have been saved had Hillary been there to help the Sno-Cats through the soft snow which he, Hillary, knew existed a few miles south of Depot 700. But Hillary had refused to accompany Fuchs from the Pole, and it made all the difference.

By Friday, February 7, Fuchs was in serious trouble, 28 miles from Depot 700. Two Sno-Cats fell into crevassed areas but both were recovered. The steering component of one was badly damaged, however, and Fuchs radioed that it would take at least five hours to repair it. Fuchs left two Sno-Cats behind and went ahead with two on a reconnaissance, but for a long time they were unable to find Hillary's trail. They radioed Scott that the leading Sno-Cat was only 7 miles from Depot 700, but with a heavily crevassed area in front of it. Hillary was all set to fly off, and could have gone at a moment's notice, but once Claydon flew him up to 700, the aircraft would have to take off within twenty minutes because of the extreme cold, and leave Hillary there alone. The aircraft could not fly out to the area in which Fuchs was stuck because of the danger of landing in crevassed areas. So Hillary had to hang on until at least one Sno-Cat arrived at 700. It was a most unfortunate delay, particularly when Fuchs radioed that the steering of still another Sno-Cat had broken. As the *Daily Mail* leading article of February 8 pertinently observed: "The Sno-Cats plunged into a crevasse in terrain which had been mapped and flagged by Sir Edmund Hillary during his dash to the Pole some six weeks ago. It seems unlikely that this particular hazard would have overtaken Fuchs if Hillary, who knows this treacherous territory, had been waiting for him in the area of Depot 700 as was originally planned."

I sometimes wonder what Hillary himself thought about this. He was certainly very edgy, and there was a most unfortunate incident directed against Mr. Bertram Jones of the *Daily Express*. In common with other members of the press, Jones, a most inoffensive man who lived in Sydney, Australia, and had flown out just before Fuchs arrived at the Pole (his first opportunity), had naturally dwelt a little on the alleged quarrel with Hillary—but I do know for a fact that what he wrote was extremely mild and in no way exaggerated.

Yet one day when Jones was walking over to Scott Base to ask the post office there to send a cable to his wife, who should he see coming towards him but the big, lumbering figure of Hillary. Without shortening his stride, Hillary shouted across to Jones: "I think you ought to know you are not particularly welcome at Scott Base!"

Somewhat taken aback, Jones, the mildest of men, stopped, and as Hillary continued walking, shouted, "What on earth for?"

Still Hillary didn't slacken his pace. He shouted: "Because I don't like all the —— you've been writing."

How utterly ridiculous in the middle of all that snow and ice! I will say that the next day Hillary sent a note of apology to Jones.

But this was not the first time that Hillary forgot his manners. He is an impulsive fellow, as quick to anger as he is good natured, and I recalled the time he had met my colleague Ralph Izzard on Everest. While the Hunt expedition (which was "tied" to *The Times* as the Fuchs expedition was) was climbing Everest, Izzard, a man of extremely good manners and much charm, brought off a real achievement by climbing in the wake of the expedition almost 18,000 feet up Everest.

Finally, incredible though it may seem, he actually caught up with them. There they were alone on the slopes of Everest and Izzard was, to say the least, inhospitably treated.

I know that on that expedition Hillary and Izzard had a row. I asked Hillary why.

"Well," replied Ed Hillary, "he had written a piece about the way we treated the Sherpas which I didn't like. It appeared in the Calcutta *Statesman* and it made me damn mad." Then he added with his schoolboy grin, "Actually I didn't know at the time, but Izzard had written quite a nice article. Those Indians had cut the good bits out and made it look critical of us."

As Fuchs approached Depot 700, and landed in trouble, the question arose again: should he call it off? He was still nearly a month behind his original plan, and the winter was closing in rapidly. A month earlier, I had written that I felt he should halt at the Pole and if possible make the second half of the journey the second year—on the presumption that, as Fuchs was a scientist and not an explorer, the glory of the achievement was secondary to the scientific value.

But at 700, all had changed, and for one very pertinent reason —the Americans had gone. Now, whether Fuchs liked it or not, this had become more than a scientific mission, more than a small part in the international grand strategy of the IGY—this was a matter of national pride for the Commonwealth. The American aircraft had left. The Pole station radio—of such enormous value to Fuchs—no longer served him. As happened when he couldn't get Scott Base in an emergency, he was cut off. No more calling up the Pole and asking them to transmit a message. No more oxygen dropped to invalids by courtesy of the American Navy. Until now Fuchs had always had the power of the U.S. Navy behind him. He had truthfully said he didn't need it. He had always been determined to stand on his own. At the Pole almost his first question had been "Where shall we pitch our tents?" and he was embarrassed by all the hospitality shown to him. Yet Fuchs had needed the Americans time and again. To get petrol in for John Lewis to fly from South Ice, because Fuchs didn't have enough. At the Pole (whether he liked it or not), for, as Griff Pugh said, his men were almost exhausted. The Pole respite of good food, a heated hut, sleep, probably made all the difference to their morale for the second half of the journey.

The same with his machines. Fuchs said his men could overhaul them in the open. But they were overhauled in the Pole garage, with much better repair facilities. The same with Geoff Pratt, when he was struck with carbon monoxide poisoning. The American Navy saved Geoff from serious and permanent illness. No doubt about it. Now Fuchs had to go on, if only to show that, with all the disasters possible, he was capable of "going it alone" and could have done so all along. The Americans were fine people, but more than one had said Fuchs would never have attempted the journey if he hadn't known the Americans were there to help. It was not true, for the expedition was planned before the IGY. But Fuchs had to show them.

There was no need to worry. Fuchs the magnificent fought his way alone inch by inch to Depot 700, and there, a burst of good weather allowed Claydon to fly Hillary up to meet him and lead him home.

The two men spent a day overhauling vehicles while John

Claydon was flying back to Scott—for the last time. The Sno-Cats were thoroughly mended, and Fuchs said that he would from now on abandon any that caused trouble, thus eliminating delays due to repair work, for each day counted now. Still, as he was taking seismic soundings at rarer intervals, he should be able to make thirty-five miles a day—especially with Hillary leading him across carefully proven paths.

At Scott we tried, even with pieces of paper and maps, to work out the exact times—accidents barred. This is how I figured it out at the time. The journey from Depot 700 was split into several stages. Firstly, there were two hundred twenty miles more across the Polar plateau to Depot 480, with some known crevassed areas to be crossed. Halfway between 700 and 480 was a small Midway Depot with an oil dump. The greatest danger on this run would be conditions changed by snowdrifts, causing new bridges hiding crevasses carefully mapped by Hillary with the precision of an old RAF navigator.

But once at 480, Fuchs expected to have a good run to 280, the Plateau Depot, at the top of the Skelton. He worked out that, with average luck, Fuchs should be at the head of the Skelton by February 23.

Then the descent of the Skelton Glacier, which Hillary told me should take four days. In case of accident, Hillary had prepared for Fuchs a detailed plan of almost every mile down the Skelton, and had given a copy of this to Admiral Dufek, who kindly loaned it to me. It brought an added touch of romantic adventuring because of its unusual place names. These were Hillary's instructions to Fuchs on leaving the Plateau Depot:

"Strike due east (True) for 11½ miles, then for about 16 miles at 110 T through the portal. Cross the neve at about 136 T. You will see Midway Nunatak on your right—a snowy, rocky shoulder—and Stepaside Spur more or less ahead. Drop down the upper staircase, keeping as close as comfortable in towards Stepaside Spur. You may see a few route-marking flags.

"On reaching the point of Stepaside Spur hug it quite closely without going up the slope, and follow it several miles round to the east. Then strike south across the landing—TO WHERE YOU SHOULD SEE SOME PETROL DRUMS AND FLAGS—spot height, 2,680. From the landing the route follows down a prominent trough winding to the left down some distance towards some exposed rock bluffs, Twin Rocks.

"Follow this trough until you emerge below Twin Rocks on long snow slopes falling in a southerly direction towards the lower rung of the glacier. Continue under CLINKER BLUFF on the bare ice of the glacier where for several miles we crossed innumerable crevasses in the ice; but it is not difficult to pick spots where they are not more than 2 feet wide if you remain down in one of the several large troughs running down the glacier.

"You will soon emerge on a flat icy surface and then 15 miles later reach the rough, windblown snow of the lower glacier. Continue centrally in the glacier until you reach the Skelton Depot at 79.03 S.—162.15 E."

Once at the foot of the Skelton, the last run home across the Ross Ice Shelf was easy, with no seismic work for the one hundred seventy miles to Scott Base. It looked as though he would catch the *Endeavour* all right, with March 10 as his latest time of arrival. But Fuchs was to beat even that date with his last burst of speed.

The two set off, with Hillary in the leading Sno-Cat. At McMurdo the ice edged in another half mile, and was actually past the camp. The airstrip looked empty and forlorn without its brightly colored aircraft. Out near a water hole a hundred or more seals lay basking in the sun, and for the first time I saw penguins—three of them—who must have followed the open water all the way from Cape Royds.

The last stage of man's last great journey on land had started. The closing chapter in a great adventure was almost to be written.

Yet it was still good news one moment, bad the next. By February 21, Fuchs was still four hundred miles from Scott Base, and on that day, the Antarctic summer sun set for the last time. From that date, the race to the coast would be undertaken in deepening twilight and increasing cold. Already a persistent whiteout had dogged them for three days, with visibility down to two hundred yards at times, reducing their daily average to 27 miles. Fuchs cabled back to London headquarters that "progress is often reduced to walking pace," and without the sun, they had to steer only by compass. Hillary was proving a tower of strength, literally "leading" Fuchs home by walking ahead on skis to mark the way with flags through the whiteout.

But in a twinkling the weather changed, the whiteouts vanished and bright sun shone on the cold world. Everything was altered. The pace was increased and in two short days, Fuchs made two great marches to reach Depot 280 by February 23—two hundred eighty miles from home and ready to start the descent of the Skelton Glacier. It was an astonishing change, and now it seemed nothing could stop him.

The weather was so good—despite the lateness of the season —that Lewis and Claydon took off in the Beaver and Otter to fly supplies to the team. Hillary had asked by radio for "fresh foods which would be a nice surprise for the boys," and going into details, listed thirteen pieces of steak, 26 fresh (frozen) eggs, seven tins of American coffee, two loaves, sliced, cooked meat, and seven tins of fruit.

The planes landed with their load, and left almost immediately taking with them two of the expedition members, Ken Blaiklock and Jon Stephenson, the dog handlers. It seemed in a way a great pity that they would not make the complete trek, but to Fuchs nothing that was not practical interested him, and they flew ahead to cut up forty seals wanted as winter food for Fuchs' dogs, which had been flown from the Pole to Scott Base.

The next stage was the Skelton Glacier—one hundred miles to Depot 180, on the edge of the ice shelf. There were only two serious crevasse areas. One was on the "staircase," a series of shallow steps leading to the Portals, a five-mile-wide scoop in the ice created by the winds which howl up to seventy miles an hour through the pass. The second was on the doorstep of Scott Base itself, where pressure ridges of ice and tidal movements had caused deep cracks. But these would never hold them back.

As Lewis said, "Nothing except extreme misfortune can stop Bunny Fuchs coming in like a shot from a gun now."

The Skelton Glacier was descended without trouble. "It was a piece of cake," said Hillary, but then, when all seemed set for the final run home across the shelf, another whiteout clamped down. As soon as they reached the Skelton Depot, at the foot of the glacier, they had to sit in their tents or Sno-Cat cabins for hours waiting for it to lift. At times the whiteout was so severe they were not able to see the ground below them from the cabs. Ralph Lenton, to whom I had talked from the Pole, radioed to Scott that the weather was too bad for Lewis to fly across the Shelf to greet them; but he said, "Spirits are high and we are looking forward to a steak and eggs homecoming supper." On February 27, Fuchs decided to strike along the shelf despite the whiteout. The orange-coloured Sno-Cats moved across the Ross Ice Shelf where Scott had perished nearly fifty years previously.

But this time no disaster struck. The whiteout lifted after several hours (as the weathermen had predicted it would) and Fuchs came across the Shelf like a bomb.

Late on Saturday night watchers from Observation Hill saw the Sno-Cats for the first time as McMurdo and Scott Bases waited *en fête* for a day that had been officially designated a public holiday. Scores of Weasels risked the ice holes to scatter across the frozen McMurdo Sound to greet the explorers as soon as they were sighted, and the sighting signal was given—a huge burst of magenta flares. The first Weasel met Fuchs still three miles to go to Scott Base, and driving in the leading Sno-Cat with Hillary, Fuchs shouted down, "We've made it! We've made it!"

The four Sno-Cats ploughed through deep snow towards the cluster of little yellow huts that is Scott Base, with the Union Jack flying in a stiff breeze. There were only a few minutes more to go through the beautiful pressure ridges in the Sound, and then through an even more difficult obstacle, the battery of photographers that surrounded them as they drew to a halt at the foot of the hill where the base is situated.

The time was 1:47 G.M.T., Sunday, March 2, 1958. The two men jumped down, all traces of disagreement gone, and Ed Hillary turned round and said, "There were times when I didn't think you would make it, Bunny, and I'm glad to have been proved wrong."

"We did what we set out to do," said Fuchs. "We never despaired though at times we met obstacles of such a nature that we wondered how they would be overcome."

Suddenly everybody was talking at the same time, when above it rose the strains of "D'ye ken John Peel" played by a scratch band from McMurdo, aided by dustbin lids. Then came the finest moment. The thirteen men walked slowly along the icy patch to the huts and the American band struck up "God Save the Queen" as the men took off their parka hoods and stood silent.

Official congratulations were exchanged, and Bunny replied: "This is not the time or the place for a long speech. I thought there might be a traffic accident in Antarctica with all these vehicles about!"

Then he read out a message from the Queen, "On the completion of your hard and adventurous journey across Antarctica my husband and I send our warmest congratulations to you and all members of the Commonwealth Trans-Antarctic Expedition. You have made a notable contribution to scientific knowledge and have succeeded in a great enterprise. Well done." With a stub of pencil, Fuchs wrote a reply,

"Our scientific work has been completed and all my party are safe. Your most gracious message has just been handed to me and my party and I am deeply appreciative of your kind words, which make complete our happiness on this day."

For the record, here are the dates of the expedition:

November 24, 1957   Started from Shackleton Base.
December 25   South Ice.

January 20, 1958	Arrived at Pole, met by Hillary, after covering 900 miles in 56 days.
February 7	Depot 700.
February 17	Depot 480.
February 27	Depot 180.
March 2	Arrived Scott Base, after 99 days. Distance 2,220 miles.

But those are cold figures and dates, and as I write this now, back in the comfort of my own home, my mind goes back to those great days and the moment that made them great as Fuchs fought his way across the white desert. The incredible personal thrill I experienced when the aircraft door opened, and I almost fell on to the hard snow and I was at the Pole; and the next day, after exploring its own particular brand of magic, talking on the radio phone —as easily as if I had been phoning London—to Ralph, Fuchs' radio operator, and hearing him say, out of the blue—or should it be out of the white?—"We've been stripped to the waist sunbathing." That strange and likable man Hillary, so different in every way from Fuchs, climbing stiffly, with his slightly shy grin, from the ridiculously small Ferguson, close to the ring of barrels that marked the site. Then back to the Pole again, and the arrival of Fuchs, the Sno-Cats with their flags flying, the dogs pulling their way by their sides, and the final splutter as the engines of the Sno-Cats stopped, and Fuchs stepped out, even then dapper in a way, after the dangers that beset them all the way up to South Ice—a trip which, as Sir James Wordie and Sir Miles Clifford in a letter to *The Times* very properly pointed out, was "A distance of 350 miles over unknown and most difficult glaciers has undoubtedly been the greatest achievement in Antarctic travel, British or otherwise."

I can see many more things in retrospect. The Pole station itself, with its orange huts half buried in the snow, and Vernon Houk, in his shirt with braces over, helping with the washing up; and Mogy, the one and only Mogy, standing with his binoculars watching the black blobs that were the Sno-Cats as they came slowly closer. That first lunch with Hillary, the grins and the shy way he talked of his exploits; and then Fuchs, pipe in hand, looking me straight in the face and saying, "Well, if we have to winter over, that's just too bad."

I like to think that these two men, each from such utterly different moulds, did, despite their differences, bring off this last great journey.

I wonder what Fuchs was thinking of as he stood there, at journey's end, listening to "God Save the Queen." Many things, the trials and tribulations, the staunch loyalty of the men who had been with him; above all, of the successful conclusion of a dream that had started nearly twenty-five years previously. I do not suppose he gave a thought to the most important thing of all: that all this would have been impossible had he not had the required determination to carry on to the end. For he fought not only the ice and the snow and the cold. He fought criticism, public opinion. I myself thought, and said, at one time, that he was crazy to carry on. Many Americans thought the same. But Fuchs plodded on, taking his seismic soundings. He never missed one, did he? Not an inch of the way, for though it might be hard to believe for one who does not know him, he genuinely, honestly, "did not make this journey for the sake of going from A to B," as he once said to me.

I don't suppose he ever did think that journey's end, successful journey's end, was due to his strange blend of courage and mysticism. He was that strangest of all men, the practical dreamer. The dream had come true, but it would never have succeeded without courage, for, as *The Times* said when he set off from Shackleton (and nobody can better its words): "Nothing has replaced courage, endurance, and accurate calculation as the indispensable equipment for a journey into these desolate regions in the face of the most savage weather in the world."

Now, it was all over. The songs and the cheering had died down, the Americans had returned from Scott to McMurdo.

Only one thing remained. Fuchs went off for a bath—his first since he left the Pole thirty-eight days previously. While he was soaking in the steaming water, still another message arrived from the Queen. It announced that he would be awarded a knighthood.

The news was kept secret until Fuchs had finished his bath. He reappeared in the small living room of Scott Base dressed in a tartan shirt and army trousers.

One of the men handed him the message as Fuchs sipped half a pint of beer.

"Good heavens!" he exclaimed.

It was exactly what Bunny Fuchs *would* say.

Diary of Events

1955

November 14: Theron sailed from London.

December 28: Theron beset in the Weddell Sea.

1956

January 23: Theron broke free of ice.

January 29: Theron arrived in Vahsel Bay. Shackleton post office established.

End of March: Nine-day blizzard which resulted in the loss of many tons of stores.

February 9 to September 15: Advance party of eight men lived in the Sno-Cat crate (21 ft. by 9 ft. by 7 ft.).

April 24: Sun left Shackleton for the winter.

June 21: Midwinter Day celebrated in the crate.

August 24: Sun returned to Shackleton. Dog training began, followed by the spring sledging journeys.

September 15: Main hut at Shackleton occupied, though not yet completed.

November 15: Magga Dan sailed from London carrying the main party.

1957

January 13: Magga Dan reached Shackleton.

January 20: Scott Base established by the New Zealand party in McMurdo Sound.

January 28: Magga Dan left Shackleton.

February 4: South Ice established by air—three men wintered there.

February 10: New Zealand party established Depot 280 at head of Skelton Glacier.

February 18: First radio contact between Shackleton and Scott Bases.

June 21: Midwinter Day celebrated at Shackleton and Scott Bases and South Ice.

October 8: South Ice relieved by air after winter, and vehicle reconnaissance party left Shackleton.

October 14: New Zealand depot-laying party left Scott Base.

November 6: New Zealand party reached Depot 280.

November 14: Reconnaissance party reached South Ice, where vehicles were left. Personnel being flown back to Shackleton.

November 24: MAIN JOURNEY BEGUN.

November 25: New Zealand party established Depot 480.

December 15: New Zealand party established Depot 700.

December 22: Main party reached South Ice.

December 25: Main party left South Ice for the Pole.

1958

January 3: New Zealand party reached the Pole.

January 19: Main party reached the Pole.

January 24: Main party left the Pole.

February 7: Main party reached Depot 700 and was joined by Sir Edmund Hillary.

February 10: Main party left Depot 700.

February 17: Main party at Depot 480.

February 23: Main party at Depot 280 (Polar plateau).

March 2: DR. FUCHS ARRIVED AT SCOTT BASE AT 2 A.M.

Members of the Trans-Antarctic Expedition

DR. VIVIAN FUCHS, aged 50, married. Between 1930 and 1932 exploring in East Africa with two separate expeditions. In 1934 led his first expedition to Lake Rudolph in Africa. Served with the Cambridgeshire Regiment during the war. Soon afterwards he was appointed leader of the Falkland Islands Dependencies Survey operating in Graham Land in Antarctica. Commenced the planning of the crossing of Antarctica in the early 1950's and sailed with the advance party in the *Theron* for the Weddell Sea in November, 1955, returning in the spring of 1956 and sailing with the main party in the *Magga Dan* in November of that year. Founders Gold Medal R.G.S. 1951, Polar Medal 1953.

KEN BLAIKLOCK, aged 29, single. Leader of advance party which wintered in the Antarctic in 1956. Spent winter of 1957 as one of a party of three at South Ice, 300 miles inland from Shackleton Base. Surveyor and dog-handler. From 1947 to 1955 was a member of the Falkland Islands Dependencies Survey; discovered Emperor Penguin rookery on Dion Islets. In 1951 was demonstrator in Polar Theatre at Festival of Britain.

DR. RAINER GOLDSMITH, aged 30, married. Member of advance party. Medical officer. Qualified at "Bart's" five years ago and served as M.O. in the P. & O. Line. Returned home in March, 1957.

FLIGHT LIEUTENANT GORDON HASLOP, aged 35, single. Flight Lieutenant, R.A.F., and second pilot of the expedition. Born in Canada, he was educated in New Zealand and joined the R.A.F. during the war. On leave from the R.A.F. Took part in first Antarctic crossing by single-engined aircraft in January, 1958.

ROY HOMARD, aged 37, married. Member of advance party. Mechanical engineer. On leave from R.E.M.E. In 1953 was a member of the British North Greenland Expedition.

PETER JEFFRIES, aged 27, single. Member of advance party. Meteorologist. Has served in the Meteorological Office and in Ocean Weather Ships. In March, 1957, was transferred to the Royal Society IGY Base at Halley Bay, Antarctica.

JOHANNES LA GRANGE, aged 30, single. Member of advance party. South African meteorologist. On leave from South African Weather Bureau.

RALPH LENTON, aged 34, single. Deputy leader of advance party. Construction engineer. From 1947 to 1955 was a member of the Falkland Islands Dependencies Survey; latterly Base leader at various F.I.D.S. Bases.

SQUADRON LEADER JOHN LEWIS, A.F.C., aged 35, married. Squadron Leader, R.A.F., and chief pilot of the expedition. On leave from the R.A.F. where, amongst other appointments, he has been an instructor at the Central Flying School. A member of the Falkland Islands Dependencies Survey Expedition with Dr. Fuchs in 1949–50. Made first Antarctic crossing by single-engined aircraft in January, 1958.

DR. HALL LISTER, aged 35, married. Glaciologist. Served in Merchant Navy and Royal Navy during the war. Subsequently studied geology at Durham University. A member of the British North Greenland Expedition in 1952–54. In charge of the party which wintered at South Ice in 1957 and which included Ken Blaiklock and Jon Stephenson.

GEORGE LOWE, O.B.E., aged 34, single. New Zealand photographer. Member of several Himalayan expeditions, including the Everest Expeditions in 1953, during which he established the last depot for Sir Edmund Hillary.

DAVID PRATT, aged 34, single. Mechanical engineer. Served in Royal Engineers during the war. Was educated at Marlborough College. Took his M.A. at Cambridge, 1952, and was occupied in development engineering in 1953–54.

GEOFFREY PRATT, aged 32, single. Geophysicist. On leave from British Petroleum Company. For the past five years has been employed by B.P.C. in the search for oil by seismic methods in Middle East, Far East, and Canada.

DR. ALLAN ROGERS, aged 40, married. Medical officer. Qualified at Bristol University and was subsequently lecturer in physiology there. Member of two Bristol High Altitude Research expeditions to the Jungfraujoch in 1953 and 1954.

DR. JON STEPHENSON, aged 27, single. Australian geologist. Studied geology at Brisbane University and in 1955 was awarded a Research Scholarship at the Imperial College in London where, until joining the expedition, he was engaged in postgraduate research in petrology. Wintered at South Ice in 1957 with Ken Blaiklock and Hal Lister.

TONY STEWART, aged 35, single. Member of advance party. Meteorologist. R.A.F. Meteorological Branch from 1944 to 1950. Master at Nautical College, Pangbourne, 1950–55. A member of Schools Exploring Society parties to Iceland, 1951 and 1952, and British Columbia in 1953. Returned home in March, 1957.

DAVID STRATTON, aged 30, married. Deputy leader. Stores officer. Surveyor and dog-handler. Educated at Harrow and Cambridge. Was in the Royal Navy Volunteer Reserve during the war. In 1951 was a member of the Swedish Glaciological Expedition to Swedish Lapland. From 1951 to 1953 was a member of the Falkland Islands Dependencies Survey and made several long sledge journeys.

FLIGHT-SERGEANT PETER WESTON, B.E.M., aged 36, married. Aircraft engineer. On leave from the R.A.F., where he has served for 19 years. A member of the Norwegian, British, and Swedish Expedition to Antarctica in 1949–52. Took part in first Antarctic crossing by single-engined aircraft in January, 1958.

SERGEANT TAFFY WILLIAMS, aged 38, single. Member of advance party. Radio engineer and operator. On leave from the R.A.F. in which he has served since 1940, his last appointment being as a Signals School Instructor. Took part in the first Antarctic crossing by a single-engined plane in January, 1958.

Members of the New Zealand Support Party

SIR EDMUND HILLARY, K.B.E.	*Leader*
BOB MILLER	*Deputy leader*
HARRY AYRES	*Mountaineer and dog-handler*
BERNIE GUNN	*Geologist*
DR. GEORGE MARSH	*Medical Officer*
MURRAY ELLIS	*Engineer*
R. A. CARLYON	*Surveyor*
LIEUTENANT F. R. BROOKE, R.N.	*Surveyor*
SQUADRON LEADER JOHN CLAYDON, R.N.Z.A.F.	*Senior pilot*
PILOT OFFICER BILL CRANFIELD, R.N.Z.A.F.	*Second pilot*
SERGEANT L. W. TARR, R.N.Z.A.F.	*Aircraft engineer*
J. E. GAWN	*Radio operator*
J. G. BATES	*Mechanic*
E. S. BUCKNELL	*Cook*
G. WARREN	*Assistant geologist*
DR. R. BALHAM	*Meteorologist*
CHIEF PETTY OFFICER P. D. MULGREW, R.N.Z.N.	*Radio operator*

Some Cold Facts About the Antarctic

THE International Geophysical Year—July 1957 to December 1958—during which more than sixty stations have been established in the Antarctic by various nations, in order to learn more about our planet, has focused world-wide attention upon the little-known continent at the bottom of the world. Actually, a great many interesting facts are known about this ice-enshrouded land.

1. Antarctica is the fifth largest continent, embracing 5,100,000 square miles of territory and equalling in size the United States and Mexico together. Having an average altitude of 6,000 feet, it is the world's highest continent.

2. The coldest temperature ever recorded was minus 102.1° F. at the U.S. South Pole Station last September 17. Prior to that time, the coldest recording at the South Pole was minus 100.4° F. on May 12, 1957. Formerly it was minus 93.6° F. at Verkhoyansk (Siberia) in 1920.

3. Fifteen minerals of potential commercial value have already been found in the Antarctic. Although no uranium-bearing ore has yet been discovered, it is felt that because Antarctica is a shield area, such deposits do exist.

4. Due to the earth's centrifugal force, objects weigh more at the Poles than they do at the Equator. This means that 5,000 tons of cargo loaded on a ship in the vicinity of the Equator would actually weigh about 50,000 pounds more at the Poles.

5. There are no polar bears or land animals in the Antarctic. Killer whales and leopard seals are the big villains in waters surrounding Antarctica. As a result, penguins and other seal species find haven on the sea ice.

6. The Antarctic contains 86 per cent of the world's glacial ice supply.

7. Great square-shaped icebergs are sloughed from the ice shelves surrounding Antarctica. One of these tabular bergs, sighted by the icebreaker U.S.S. *Glacier* between the Antarctic Continent and New Zealand on November 12, 1956, was 208 miles long and 60 miles wide, approximately the size of Connecticut.

8. An atmospheric condition known as a "whiteout" is a frequent Antarctic occurrence and endangers both plane and trail operations. Aviators say it is like flying in a bowl of milk. Loss of horizon and shadows, which give perspective, is caused by reflected light.

9. In spite of its being a land of ice and snow, the Antarctic Continent is the home of a large, active volcano, 13,000-foot-high Mount Erebus, which is located in the McMurdo Sound area.

10. The intense cold and sterility of Antarctic air preserves food and materials almost indefinitely. For instance, corned beef, canned beans, and sugar cached by the Swedish explorer, Nordenskjold, provided a most satisfactory meal for the British Falkland Islands Dependencies Survey party forty-five years later. The print on a magazine, too, was as readable as ever.

11. The Antarctic Seas, scientists contend, produce more food per acre than anywhere else in the world, on land or sea. Most of this is in the form of diatoms, microscopic plants on which small shrimps ("red krill"—*Euphausia superba*) feed. Some day in the future, this source of food may be of great value to the human race.

12. They mine for water at the South Pole. Since the only water available is that which can be melted from snow, and low temperatures frequently prevent sustained activity outside, water for the International Geophysical Year station at the South Pole is being obtained from germ-free snow blocks dug from a snow mine, directly reached from the station living quarters.

13. People may have lived at one time in the Antarctic. In 1893, Captain Larsen, the Norwegian sealer, found about 50 clay balls, perched on pillars of the same material on Seymour Island off the eastern coast of the Palmer Peninsula. "These," he reported, "had the appearance of having been made by human hands."

14. Recently an airfield in McMurdo Sound, Antarctica, was repaired by use of a mixture consisting of snow, ice, and water. During a midsummer hot spell, the ice runway began to melt in areas where waste and oil had collected. Refreezing was successfully accomplished by filling the chuckholes with the mixture and allowing the colder evening temperatures to do their work more efficiently.

15. Penguins and other Antarctic birds are being captured by the hundreds through use of a cannon-hurled net. Carl Eklund, ornithologist and leader at the U.S. Wilkes Station, is banding these birds with various coloured plastic leg bands in order to learn their migratory habits.

16. Diametrically opposite geographically, the Arctic and Antarctic are opposite in other ways, too. The Antarctic is land surrounded by water, whereas the Arctic is water surrounded by land. This accounts for the colder temperatures of Antarctica. The South Pole rests on a polar plateau of about 10,000 feet altitude, whereas the North Pole is in the middle of a sea about 10,000 feet deep.

17. Rear Admiral Dufek, in October, 1956, was the first man after Norway's Amundsen party (December, 1911) and England's Scott party (January, 1912) to set foot on the South Geographical Pole. At that time a Navy plane landed to start preliminary operations on setting up a scientific station for the eighteen men now manning this camp at the foot of the world during the IGY.

18.   In spite of two large grounded icebergs, one 34 miles long and the other 27 miles long, which delayed the two-ship Weddell Sea expedition, the U.S.S. *Staten Island* and the U.S.S. *Wyandot,* Navy icebreaker and cargo ship, reached over 300 miles further into the Weddell Sea than any other ship in history.

19.   Seismograph readings during 1957 at Byrd Station in Marie Byrd Land show that the IGY station may be resting on ice which extends from 5,000 feet below sea level to 5,000 feet above sea level.

20.   Captain Nathaniel Palmer, an American from Stonington, Connecticut, was probably the first man to sight the Antarctic Continent. This took place on November 17, 1820, when the *Hero,* in search of fur seals, sailed close to the peninsula (now named after him) in the vicinity of Trinity Island. Captain John Davis, also an American, was thought to be the first to actually land, on February 7, 1821, at Hughes Bay on the peninsula. The British, however, do not subscribe to these views, and call the peninsula in question Graham Land, after one of their own early Antarctic backers. They base their claims to discovery on a chart prepared by the British explorer, Edward Bransfield, in 1820.

21.   Oceanography will help reveal the geological composition of Antarctica. Core samples of sediment dredged up from the sea in the canyons of prehistoric Antarctic rivers are likely to show the true make-up of the Antarctic Continent, because these rivers once carried Antarctic silt into the sea.

22.   Due to the earth's rotation, ice drifts to the left of the wind in the Antarctic, whereas it drifts to the right in the Northern Hemisphere. Likewise, persons who have become lost find they circle to the left in the Antarctic and to the right in the Arctic.

23.   Antarctica once had a tropical climate. Numerous fossil tropical ferns and plant-life have been found embedded in rock on the Palmer Peninsula.

24.   The round, barrel-shaped hulls of the Navy icebreakers prevent them from ever becoming crushed in Antarctic ice. Their peculiar construction enables them to pop up like peas in a pod if pressure reaches dangerous proportions. DeLong's *Jeannette,* crushed and trag-

ically lost in the Arctic near the end of the last century, possessed the conventional perpendicular, straight-sided hull.

25. Antarctica, once a land of lush vegetation with a temperate or even semi-tropical climate, may have been part of a huge southern continent. Gondwanaland, as it is called, supposedly contained what is now known as Africa, South America, Australia, New Zealand, parts of India, and Antarctica. Proponents of Gondwanaland, or the continental drift theory, maintain that ages ago the continents drifted on a fluidlike subterranean layer of the earth to their present locations.

26. Want fizz water? Put a chip of ice from an Antarctic iceberg into your drink. The entrapped air makes a popping sound when it is released on melting.

27. Penguins (of which the Antarctic has hundreds of thousands), it is believed, have difficulty ascertaining each other's sex. This is overcome during the mating season by the simple expedient of the male offering a small rock to his intended. If accepted, it's a good bet that the recipient is a female.

28. That the earth was hollow and habitable with entry to the outside world somewhere in the Antarctic was a popular belief in the United States early in the 19th Century. Jeremiah N. Reynolds, chief proponent of this view, was so convincing that no less than 20 bills were introduced in Congress proposing that a Navy expedition sail into the globe's interior.

29. Antarctic skua gulls entertain no fear of man. Numerous instances of these eagles of the Antarctic diving on individual explorers have been recorded. Choice morsels for these fierce birds are penguin chicks and eggs.

30. The International Geophysical Year has special significance as it applies to the Antarctic. The scientists of 12 nations at 62 Antarctic stations are currently gathering data in the fields of meteorology, aurora and air glow, glaciology, cosmic rays, gravity and seismology, ionospheric physics, and geomagnetism. Clarity of atmosphere and periods of sustained darkness render observations taken in the Antarctic extremely valuable.

31. Upon departure of the U.S.S. *Wyandot* for Antarctica in November, 1956, two young women on the dock held aloft a sign, reading, "Is This Trip Necessary?"

32. The peculiar ice shelves of the Antarctic, from which tabular, block-shaped icebergs are born, are the result of the Antarctic glacial cap pushing itself beyond the limits of the land. One such ice barrier, the Ross Ice Shelf, occupies a water area about equal to the State of California.

33. The existence of Antarctica as a continent was not known until the middle of the 19th century, when Lieutenant (later Rear Admiral) Charles Wilkes, U.S. Navy, sailed halfway around it. The many landfalls seen by this expedition first determined the continental dimensions of Antarctica.

34. The Commonwealth Bay area in the Antarctic is believed to be the windiest region in the world. The mean velocity for July, 1913 was 55.6 miles per hour. During the month of August, 1913, average velocity of 80.6 miles an hour was recorded over a 24 hour period, with gusts momentarily reaching over 100 miles per hour. The calmest month was February, 1912, with an average velocity of 26.2 miles per hour.

35. Bills for the creation of a permanent Antarctic Institute or Commission (to be known as the Richard E. Byrd Commission) in the United States have recently been introduced in both Houses of Congress. Their purpose is to foster and maintain continued American interest in the Antarctic.

36. Rear Admiral Richard E. Byrd, our late great polar explorer, was not only the first to fly over the South Pole, but was the first to live alone in the Antarctic. For five long, weary months, often ill from fumes from the stove, he lived in a small snow-covered hut, religiously taking weather and temperature readings, sometimes with outside temperatures ranging to about 80° F. below zero. During all this time, his only contact with other humans was by a small hand-cranked radio to Little America, 123 miles distant.

37. Objects hundreds of miles away sometimes may be seen clearly by the naked eye in the Antarctic. This peculiarity, known as looming, may have been responsible for a portion of sightings by early Antarctic

explorers. It is brought about by an atmospheric condition which meteorologists term an inversion; warmer layers of air exist above colder ones
and cause light rays from the object to the eye to be curved concavely
downward towards the earth's surface.

38. Two American women, Mrs. Edith Ronne and Mrs. Jennie
Darlington, of Washington, D.C., participating in the Finn Ronne
expedition of 1947–48, were the first women ever to spend a winter on
the Antarctic Continent. With the original intention of returning to
the United States from a South American port, both then decided to
accompany their husbands aboard the expedition ship, *The Port of
Beaumont*, on the voyage south to Antarctica.

39. In their race to the South Pole, Roald Amundsen of Norway,
setting out by dog team from his base, Framheim, in the Bay of Whales
area (near the site of Little America I), reached the coveted goal on
December 14, 1911. England's famed polar explorer, Captain Robert
Scott, hindered by the initial use of Siberian ponies, greater distances,
unfavorable weather, and necessity to finally man-haul the sleds, ulti-
mately attained the Pole from the McMurdo Sound area on January
12, 1912. On the long journey back, Scott and his three companions
perished.

40. During the present International Geophysical Year, Antarctica, in spite of claims made, is regarded as a free area by all participating nations. This principle has always been observed by the United
States. It has never officially recognized the claims put forth by other
nations but has reserved all its rights in the Antarctic.

41. The first man to drop on the South Pole by parachute was
Air Force Technical Sergeant Richard J. Patton, who volunteered for
the feat in the hope of learning why some cargo parachutes carrying
equipment had failed to open.

42. The Antarctic region is usually regarded as that region en-
closed by the Antarctic convergence, a twenty- to thirty-mile-wide zone
in the sea where the cold, northward-flowing Antarctic waters sink beneath the warmer waters of the sub-Antarctica.

43. The mammoth, rubber-tired "Snow Cruiser," transported to
Antarctica on Rear Admiral Byrd's 1939–41 expedition, was no doubt

the most interesting vehicle ever designed for polar travel. Its wheels could be raised into compartments inside so that it was able to slide down ridges on its belly runners. It even carried a small plane on its roof. Besides living quarters for four men, it contained a machine shop, laboratories, and photographic and long-range radio facilities. Originally scheduled for the long overland snow trip to the South Pole and return, its power proved wholly inadequate and it never left Little America.

44. About 12,000 men, mainly from the countries of the British Commonwealth, Japan, Norway, and the U.S.S.R., go into Antarctic waters each year to hunt the whale. Besides the oil derived from these kills, the bone and meat are utilized to provide additional profit.

45. Colonize Antarctica? This is a question often asked. Proponents of Antarctic colonization say that coal deposits there would provide heat and power, and a large proportion of the food could be derived from the sea. Vegetables also could be produced in chemically treated water (hydroponics) during the long summer season. The isolation and rigorous climate, not to mention the tremendous cost of outside support involved, may, however, discourage permanent colonization on this cold land mass.

46. In 1901 the first and only captive balloon ascension was made on the Antarctic Continent in the Ross Sea sector. England's Scott went up almost 800 feet to observe what lay beyond the ice barrier to the south.

47. For the present International Geophysical Year, the United States has established five scientific stations, one scientific logistics station, and one joint scientific station (with New Zealand). These are located at: Kainan Bay (Little America V), Marie Byrd Land (Byrd), South Pole (Amundsen-Scott), Knox Coast (Wilkes), Weddell Sea (Ellsworth), McMurdo Sound (McMurdo), and Cape Hallet (Hallet).

48. For the International Geophysical Year, Soviet Russia has established four bases, two coastal and two inland, in the Queen Mary coast sector (claimed by Australia). The Soviets have announced intentions to erect two additional inland stations and effect coastal landings in the Amundsen and Bellingshausen Sea areas during the 1957–58 season. These latter areas are not claimed at present by any nation.

Personal Postscript

THIS book is ended and it is for my son Bengy, and I would say but this for him to read when he is of age:

> I dedicate it to my son who is only three years old; and from whom I am parted on voyages of excitement too frightening or too glorious for me to resist; but each one tears part of my heart away for I hate to be parted from him; and since he will one day be a man, I like to think that he will understand what is so hard to understand: that man is not only yes or no, hard or soft, sentimental or cynical, but a mixture, and that I, with all my faults, love to dream, and cannot help but dream, as I work for my living, and fight for my living; and in Antarctica I lived through its greatest drama and I did not leave the white desert untouched or unmoved by what I saw.